Roy Kunda

King of the Cape

The Guide's Book to your
Ultimate Motorcycling Adventure

First published by Ultimate World Publishing 2020
Copyright © 2020 Roy Kunda

ISBN

Paperback - 978-1-922372-56-7
Ebook - 978-1-922372-57-4

Roy Kunda has asserted his right under the Copyright, Designs and Patents Act 1988 to be identified as the author of this work. The information in this book is based on the author's experiences and opinions. The publisher specifically disclaims responsibility for any adverse consequences, which may result from use of the information contained herein. Permission to use information has been sought by the author. Any breaches will be rectified in further editions of the book.

All rights reserved. No part of this publication may be reproduced, stored in or introduced into a retrieval system, or transmitted in any form, or by any means (electronic, mechanical, photocopying, recording or otherwise) without the prior written permission of the author. Any person who does any unauthorised act in relation to this publication may be liable to criminal prosecution and civil claims for damages. Enquiries should be made through the publisher.

Cover design: Ultimate World Publishing
Layout and typesetting: Ultimate World Publishing
Editor: James Salmon
Front Cover photo: Andrew "Clubby" Clubb.
Back Cover photo: Philip Warring; "PhlipVids".

Ultimate World Publishing
Diamond Creek,
Victoria Australia 3089
www.writeabook.com.au

Testimonials

"The King of the Cape"..."Robert De Niro of the North"... he also goes by a few less flattering names but most just know him as Roy. His wife Renae people mostly just call 'Renae'. They're both known from Cairns to the Cape and between the two of them they've built an incredible business and added so much to so many people's enjoyment, appreciation and understanding of Australia's Cape York.

Like the red dust of the Cape, the experience of a Cape York trip with Cape York Motorcycle Adventures is indelibly etched into you. You don't lose it. I had the pleasure of many trips with CYMCA and their crew – as a private customer, later magazine editor, sometimes track explorer – and every time I left my main thought was, "When can I do that again?". Especially that one time Roy speared off the track trying to take me on the inside. I'd do that again any day!

30 years is a helluva milestone Roy & Renae. Congratulations. The stories in this book couldn't come close to all the memories and yarns...look forward to sharing a few unpublished ones around a fire one day soon.

Cheers, Ross Elliott.
PS: Roy, I've still never seen you actually catch a barra.

I worked for Roy full time for six years as a tour guide/mechanic. Anyone with a pulse would say that it is a dream job and it was but it also involved a lot of hard work, cleaning and servicing bikes and support vehicles to ensure the punters (customers) are having a good time and aren't pushing themselves beyond their abilities. Roy's relaxed/down-to earth nature made it easy for me to learn how to be good at this job.

Roy was a master of staying calm when things turned pear-shaped. Whether it was crossing a seemingly impassable, flooded river or extracting a broken bike (or person) out of a remote location Roy would always do it with such a relaxed and professional manner that put the customers at ease. He made it look as if it were all part of the show.

If you ever go on tour with him ask for some of Roy's crazy damper (or crazy Roy's damper ha, ha). I had an awesome experience working for Roy and still do occasional work for him to this day. I consider the Kunda's more as family then friends!

**Lincoln McKay,
Lincs Moto & Small Engines.**

TESTIMONIALS

I may be a little biased towards CYMCA but in short, my first experience was only two months after first riding a motorcycle. Roy I wouldn't say pushed me, more encouraged me to ride within my own ability, and I made it to the tip. In the years to follow, I returned again and again, riding, fishing and living life to the fullest. Roy and Renae I regard now as family, when I am above the Daintree River I live a life away from phones, emails and simply enjoy life. It's not a bucket list item, it's a must do item.

**Mark Petersen,
Managing Director - Troy Bayliss Events.**

In 2016 and 2017 I worked as a tour guide with Roy, In that time I soon learned how passionate Roy is about his tours, ensuring that each and every customer goes home with a memory of a lifetime. Cheers mate for the opportunity, laughs and challenges you gave me, bloody legend, next wild turkey is on me!

Regards, Mark Newth.

Dedication

I dedicate this book to firstly my wife, Renae, for I would never have written it without her persuasion, and to my children for their inspiration and my family for their support.

Disclaimer:

Roy and Renae Kunda have asserted their right under the Copyright, Designs and Patents Act 1988 to be identified as the author of this work. We have tried to recreate events, locales and conversations from our memories of them. In order to maintain their anonymity in some instances we have changed the names of individuals and places, we may have changed some identifying characteristics and details.

The information in this book is meant to complement, not replace, proper motorcycle rider training. Like any sport involving speed, equipment, balance and environmental factors, motorcycling poses inherent risk. The authors and publisher advise readers to take full responsibility for their safety and know their limits. Before practicing the skills described in this book, be sure that your equipment is well maintained, and do not take risks beyond your level of experience, aptitude, training, and comfort level.

The information provided in this book is designed to provide helpful information on the subjects discussed. This book is not meant to be used, nor should it be used as a standalone tool for education purposes. The authors and publisher are not liable for any damages or negative consequences from any action, application or preparation, to any person reading or following the information in this book. Readers should also be aware that the websites listed in this book may change.

The contents of this book may not be used in any lawsuits or litigation, be reproduced, edited or distributed or used in any other way unless you have written permission of the author.

Contents

Dedication	vii
Introduction	1
Chapter 1: Because I said so	5
Chapter 2: Be honest	11
Chapter 3: The people you meet	19
Chapter 4: Take yourself	29
Chapter 5: Traps for young players	41
Chapter 6: Horses for courses	53
Chapter 7: Customising	59
Chapter 8: Shit happens	71
Chapter 9: Dress for the occasion	89
Chapter 10: Techniques	95
Chapter 11: The anchor	107
Chapter 12: Less is more	117
Chapter 13: Lifelines	127
Afterword	135
About the Author	139
Testimonials Part 2	145

Introduction

During the process of writing this book a few people asked me if I was retiring and so I want to start out by saying, "Absolutely NOT". I love what I do and I have no intentions of giving up riding EVER! In fact, I want to expand and add some different locations to our tour offering, so my regular clients have somewhere new to explore. I don't mind exploring new areas myself so that's what we will be doing more of.

I love riding motorbikes and challenging myself to improve my skill set. I'm not as young as I used to be nor am I as gung-ho as I used to be and the challenges are more mental to keep my brain and reaction times sharp. Adventure riding, to me, is all about finding beautiful and secluded locations, discovering what rare activities it has to offer; firstly am I going to find a new secret fishing spot? Will it have a blue lagoon or hidden spring to swim? When I get to the end of this new road am I going to see a spectacular sight? What test lays before me and what do I have to do to get there? The saying you can't teach an old dog new tricks couldn't be more wrong in this book – if the dog wants to learn! I've taught myself many new tricks and I've watched a lot of old dogs learning. The patience and wisdom of the old dog is sometimes easier to teach than the bouncing pup.

It's not all about the riding though – I would say that more than half of the best times we have are while we are sitting around a campfire, meeting new people along the way and finding the things that we have in common that will develop long-term friendships. The best way I know to do that is to spend some time together, share some experiences and have a beer to chat about it at the end of the day.

I like the idea of meeting people from all over the world, it's a real buzz for me to watch them take in what they're doing for the first time. Some of the individuals I've met have never been outside of a big city. They're out of their depth in those first couple of days and then the wonder creeps up slowly on their faces as they relax into the quiet moments, take in the scenery and realise how far from home they really are.

They've never camped or slept out under the stars; they've never bathed in a creek or taken a spa in a waterfall. They've never caught their own food and seen it cooked on a fire. They've definitely never had to worry about the ice melting in the esky and the drinks going warm. They've never been outside of their comfort zone and I love to watch their whole perception of the world change. That's the biggest part of the job for me and that's what keeps me going – the people.

I love the Cape. It's been surprising me for 35 years but I can't tell you all my stories – some are highly illegal and some are just downright gory, so we might save those for the next book after a lawyer has written a really good indemnity. And besides, I have to save some things for those moments when I'm sitting around the campfire with a new group of mates, icy bourbon in hand and while the armchair racing is on. Oh, armchair racing is when we

INTRODUCTION

sit around the campfire and talk about the events of the day and the rider's recollection blows out of proportion.

I've told a lot of my stories at these race events around the campfire and it's always interesting to watch people laugh and not believe me. I have the hardest time convincing them that it was an actual event that happened in my life. When I tell them a second and a third experience that I've had in my life and back it up with an explanation, of why I do what I do and why I say what I say, by using an example that happened today they tend to go quiet as the doubt seeps away. Then nine times out of ten they will say, "Roy, you have to write a book". My wife, Renae has always agreed and has been on my case for years to get the stories out of my head and onto the page. Then the Covid-19 pandemic forced us all indoors and I had nowhere to go!

I sat down next to Renae and we reminisced, we laughed a lot and she cried at times but continued to type the memories as I recited them – of course she edited them into sentences and paragraphs later. I had a really hard time reading it for the first time. I looked at Renae and said, "I sound like I'm totally up myself, I don't want to do this".

So just to clarify I am in fact a very private person and pretty shy, it takes me a little while to open up to people outside of my domain and that's what I'm speaking about in this book. I'm a little fish in a big pond and I know it. There are far better riders than me, there are far better mechanics than me. However, I'm fairly certain no-one has done the same miles on a motorcycle in Cape York as I have and so I kept going.

It is really hard to tell a story about myself without sounding a little bit self-centred and I hope you can read through those moments and remember that I am a humble guy and that my wife made me write this book. Just like every one of you would be – I am nervous to be criticised for what I say here but if riding bikes has taught me anything it is to be bold in the face of fear.

Most of the stories taught me big lessons and it's through those learnings that I've gained my experience and it's why I do what I do. It is my hope that you will gain a better understanding of the hazards and pitfalls that surround an adventure ride. I hope that by reading my stories you will be able to create the picture and see firsthand how these things can and do actually happen. If it stays in your mind and helps you to predict where it might happen to you and you have a split second to prevent it then it will all be worth it for me.

For the purposes of this book and for privacy reasons the names of the people have been changed.

I'm going to put the stories in italics, for those of you who are not technically minded or have no intention of using this book to seek out a motorcycle adventure, so that you can skip to the parts of the book that have funny stories and events. For the rest of you who want to learn a few of the tips and tricks then the whole book is for you.

CHAPTER 1

Because I said so

The sand python[1]

I see them ALL the time. I came up with this saying when I was riding out in the middle of a remote part of Cape York, in that sweet humming zone, just me and the bike. I was enjoying the sceneries that settled before me when the sharp point of a tail carved in the trail caught my eye. Just as I started to find the zone again I noticed a shoe, just one, and that's kind of odd out there. A little further along and a single, curved belly print formed in the sand. It was quickly followed by a sleeping bag in the grass alongside the trail. My attention was starting to focus on the unfolding treasure hunt. Another big 'S' in the sand that looked like a python just slid through here moments earlier and boy was he a big one. Another odd item. This went on until the creature appeared – he was exhausted, dehydrated and laying on the ground in the shade. His motorcycle lay close by and he appeared to have no intention of picking up that lump of metal in the middle of the trail. It was heavy that's for

---
[1] Sand Python – A rider that is fatigued and swerving all over the road.

sure, way too heavy for this track. It was over packed and top heavy – no wonder he was weaving his way like a python through the sand.

So I helped Sandy up, checked him over for injuries, offered him water and a few words of encouragement. He slowly came to life and I found out that he bought the bike in Sydney and had ridden about 3000 km's to where I found him, out in the middle of nowhere. He was a smaller guy and had the bike loaded up to the hilt with enough gear to build a house but nothing that was practical for his survival in this remote area. The little army bottle of water he had on board probably held a litre, if that.

Sandy hadn't done any maintenance since departing Sydney, had travelled most of his kilometres on the road and was heading for the tip of Cape York. His chain was that loose that it was nearly dragging on the ground, his tyre pressure was rock hard and his gearing was stock standard and totally wrong for these conditions. He had everything going against him because he hadn't set up the bike to personalise and maximise his ride experience and it's these small things that people overlook all the time. Sandy just didn't know any better and he'd taken on a really big adventure ride without the experience to achieve his goal.

Let me point out a few things here. Adjusting your chain on a regular basis will ensure a smoother power delivery and ride and it minimises the wear and tear on the chain and sprockets. If you have it too tight, you will run the risk of excess wear leading to an inevitable link breakage. If you have it too loose, the response becomes jerky and the chain is more likely to derail off the sprockets.

Along with all these errors on the machine, Sandy was also a very green off-road rider who hadn't done any research on the area that he wanted to go to! He'd looked at a map that would take him from point 'A' to point 'B' and it all looked easy enough – but that map didn't explain the condition differences between travelling on the highway from Sydney to Cairns as opposed to the matching kilometres of remoteness between Cairns and the tip of Cape York. Make sure you know your facts and factors about the area you want to travel. The map doesn't explain the road conditions, it doesn't tell you the rain expectations for the time of year you are travelling, or what the likely temperatures will be. It will tell you where you can buy fuel but it won't tell you the variation differences that you will use between on-road highway riding and weaving your way through the trails like a sand python. The economy you would get out of a motorcycle on a wide open highway is vastly different to what you will achieve on a sandy Cape York Highway but they both look the same on that map. Now I am not saying that you have to be an expert to enjoy adventure riding but you do have to set yourself up for success and design your challenges so that they are achievable.

Most people are watching inspiring riders on television or at race meetings or wherever it is that you get your inspirations from. They're doing amazing things and you think you can copy their techniques and improve your skill level. Let me tell you if you go out there trying to mimic Toby Price in the hope that there may be a chopper chasing you to film it, it is likely going to see you end up in hospital. Start with the baby steps! You might look like a wood duck rider for a time but who cares if you get through to that dream destination unscathed, I mean, isn't that the point after all! Save the stress and EGO for the race track, we're here to ride and to see and experience the beautiful things in life. When you start your day, imagine the campfire tonight with a cold beer in hand, it makes the ride much more enjoyable.

I see these things all the time and I will be covering more in-depth issues in later chapters so that you can have a better understanding of things that most people overlook when preparing for their adventure trip! Let's make your experience the best it can be, let's make it enjoyable and trouble free. Let's take a lesson from the sand python and recap: knowledge, learn everything you can about the map between your point 'A' and 'B' and practice your fuel range beforehand if you can – double-check how much fuel you are going to need. Don't over pack and make your bike top heavy, it's just hard work. Know your bike and customise it for your adventure. Self-preservation is key; ride to your limits – it's a holiday, not a race.

I've got to add this little memory or Renae won't forgive me – she thinks it's the funniest story she's ever heard. So I was travelling around Australia with my good friend 'Dundee' – he got that name because he's always worn a cowboy hat ever since I've known him, even when we were kids living in Melbourne. In fact, I don't think I've ever seen his legs outside of a pair of jeans either. I have the biggest respect for my mate Dundee, he's quietly spoken if he speaks at all and he's the handiest bushy[2] you'll ever meet. So we were riding around with all of our worldly possession strapped to our bikes and camping out in swags on the ground every night. Now you have to realise that I sleep with my hands tucked up cradling

---

[2] Bushy – A handy bushman that knows how to survive in remote areas

my head because we didn't carry pillows on the bike and sometimes my arms freeze up through the night. Have you ever had that feeling when your arms don't work or you just can't feel anything but pins and needles? That's where I was at, tucked up in my sleeping bag in the middle of the night and thinking the zip was flapping in the breeze a bit and tickling my chest. Through the cramp, I loosely wiggled my fingers over it to try to remove the irritation. I'm a pretty heavy sleeper so I don't wake easily but I registered that my sleeping bag was a bit heavy and I was starting to feel really uncomfortable, so I had to force my eyes open if I wanted to get back to sleep. In the moonlight I saw a foreign object – it was coiled up and unmoving when it dawned on me that it was a snake using me as a hot water bottle. Well back then I wasn't real keen on snakes so I was bolt upright on my feet in the blink of an eye and the snake fell into the hole I'd made in my swag. My bloody arms wouldn't work and in that moment I thought I'd been boa-constricted by this massive snake. Flapping like an idiot trying to get the snake out of my bag, I noticed Dundee take a glance and laugh as if nothing had happened, but he gave me 'that look' so I noted that I'd rudely woken him and the rest of the campsite up. It made me feel like a bit of city slicker let me tell ya. Anyway, we moved on the next day and about a week later we rocked into a pub one night for dinner. Sitting at the bar having a beer and waiting for our number to be called we heard this guy telling his mate a story about the lady who woke up with a python in her swag and how she was jumping around and squealing and waking the whole camp. Well, I never heard Dundee laugh so hard, spurting his mouthful of beer across the bar when he realised they were talking about me! Bloody pythons, I'm not scared of them anymore, I wasn't going to let that happen again!

CHAPTER 2

Be honest

The DIVE instructor

On the first day of every tour I've ever done I like to go around and get to know the group while they are getting ready and putting on their riding gear. After finding out their names and where they are from the first real question I ask each rider is, "How much experience do you have off-road?".

On this particular day we had a group of novices that had spent most of their time riding on-road, some had a little experience off-road and Dave answered that he was a riding instructor. "Excellent," I thought. "I don't have to worry about you."

We cruised nice and easy to the first river crossing. Here, I stopped the group and asked them to wait until I checked the creek for water height and checked the bottom as I took my bike to the other side. There were a few boulders that hiccupped the bike but nothing major underfoot. On *the other side there was a rather ominous hill climb directly in sight but we could take a slight, right-hand, uphill curve to navigate out of the water safely. The uphill bank was made up of loose mulchy matter that meant it required a bit of momentum to make it to the top. It was a bit of a challenge but nothing too dramatic. I parked my bike out of the way then walked back halfway across the creek. I signalled for the first rider to come towards me and waved my hands down in a motion to gesture, 'steady, steady'. One after the other they all struggled through – my guides and I helped them across the creek.*

Little did I know at the time that Dave was watching on in horror, watching all of his mates, one by one drop the bike and struggle to get up this bank. He was nervous, so nervous that his electrical system shorted out any brain activity that he might have once had. It was his turn and all he knew how to do was turn the throttle! The bike hit its first boulder and bucked. His feet were off the pegs and his legs flapped out like spaghetti, Dave still had a firm grip on the bars and that throttle opened up even more. I watched him head to the exit turn that never happened and there was nothing I could do! He went straight up the 90 degree incline, never letting go of the throttle. The bike now had one wheel in the air and pivoted 180 degrees on the rear, and he still had a firm grip on those bars and the throttle. His right hand was locked solid in a classic 'throttle freeze'[3] moment. As the bike reared and spun towards me I could see the whites of Dave's eyes through his goggles as he had turned back to face me standing in the water. The front wheel came back down in what seemed like slow motion towards the water. As it did, he finally let go and assumed the diving posture with his hands out in a superman pose and glided elegantly over the top of the bars and into the river. The dive instructor! Little did I know that he taught ON-ROAD riding only!

So this little creek crossing seemed more technical than he thought but it really wasn't, it's something he could have easily ridden through had he just kept his cool, didn't overthink it and just rode with the skills

---

[3] Throttle Freeze – Holding the throttle open when you should let go.

BE HONEST

he had. Watching the majority of novice riders ahead of him making mistakes or having troubles, Dave panicked and psychologically made it all a lot more difficult for himself than it really was.

As a guide we have to do a degree in psychology to find out what headspace our riders are in and judge what information they need to know right now – or perhaps we just need to check their heart rates at each technical section. The outsides can be deceiving. When you spend a week or more with a fella you get to know him pretty well and after the years I've spent doing this I have developed a knack for spotting the ones who might need a little extra help here and there. It's been the longest degree in psychology anyone has ever done but now I can spot that fella a mile away.

The classic example that makes up a large majority of our riders are the professional men or small business entrepreneurs who gave up bikes to concentrate on a career or the wife and kids. He hasn't ridden for ten or 20 years or more and he's just got that itch to get out there and do it again. Here he is getting on for the first time and he feels just like he did when he was a young buck, he's all in a rush to have a good time. He forgets that he's on a multi-day tour and that there's a long way to go. We call this 'first day fever[4]', he starts off and is having such a great time and it's all coming back to him. He's psyching himself up, gaining confidence and speed and congratulating himself on not losing his skills from the past. He starts to push those boundaries and tries harder and faster with each small challenge he encounters.

All of a sudden the upcoming corner doesn't match the last ten he just blasted through. This one has a switchback that catches him out – thankfully it was just the trail and not an oncoming vehicle that greets him and he's smart enough to know this too. He runs off the trail and into the scrub, finding his limit as fast as he did when he

---

[4] First Day Fever – Being in a rush to have a good time and not using your brain

was a young fella. For every action there is an equal and opposite reaction, and this guy, instead of picking himself up and dusting himself off and getting on with the job having just learned the big lesson, completely shuts down and totally loses his confidence. He's super slow, overthinking every pattern or skill and he becomes a worse rider than he was at the beginning of the day. He's totally spooked and that's where we step in with that degree and guide him back with small encouragements.

Don't be in a rush to have a good time, take your time and be there at the end.

Standing right next to him is the guy who organised the trip, the highly experienced rider and leader of the pack. He's been arranging the rides for his mates every weekend for years and he finally gets them all organised for the adventure of a lifetime. Everyone is here and ready to start their tour of Cape York. So I ask him the question, "How much experience do you have off-road?". He lets me know with a hearty huffed laugh that he's been organising this group for years, claiming that they all follow him because he used to race back in the day. This guy is so focused and so excited that he can't wait to show off his experience and skills to his mates – and to the guides for that matter. After everyone is geared up we do a guide's briefing for the day ahead. We point out everything they will encounter today, the things they need to be aware of and particularly warn them about 'first day fever', which comes in so many different forms. After our briefing, I ask if there are any questions and the big fella steps up to do **his** briefing for **his** riders, repeating some but not all of the things we've just tried to plant in their heads.

He then enthusiastically takes the group out to the bikes for the group photograph before we've even run through the bikes in any detail, so we round them all back up and start the mechanical briefing. This is when we would normally do the group photo

– when the boys and girls are ready to jump on for a quick ride around to familiarise themselves with their mount. When everyone looks comfortable and settled with the bikes we head out along the driveway toward the highway. I'm out front and judge a good distance to join the traffic that's traveling at 100 kilometres per hour. A quick glance in the rear vision mirror scares the beejezus out of me – the big fella is so excited to get started that he just follows without hesitation OR A SIDEWARDS GLANCE at the traffic. Without even looking he leads his whole bunch of mates out there with him. There are cars screeching to a halt cursing and swerving to avoid a collision. The big fella and his group are the only ones on the road that matter in this very moment.

Having ridden your whole life in one area and having expert experience in that area doesn't make you an experienced rider all-round. This guy has ridden his whole life in Victoria and around the high country. That used to be me so I can see this fella a mile away. He is an expert – it is true he's a great rider but he's an expert in his own experience. He doesn't know any different but throw in a few altered terrains that he hasn't experienced before, like bulldust, and he's out of his league – but his ego is not.

We were riding through Lakefield National Park when we experienced numerous (small and fairly safe) bulldust patches. Let's not forget that I've been doing this for a while so I know that if I pull the boys up too early they won't take in what I'm about to tell them, but if I wait a little bit and let them get a taste of it out of the blue then for sure they will take it all in. So, I explained to the guys what bulldust is and what to look for. Once your eyes are trained you can spot these holes coming up. Bulldust is a fine dust that settles in and conceals dangerous potholes, it has a variation in colour because it's not solid. If you disturb the hole it will spew up forming a choking volcano of cloud that can completely reduce any visibility.

KING OF THE CAPE

Your best bet is to either get through it slow and steady because you won't know what's underneath this powder or to avoid it all together if you can go around it. On this day we moved on, and after a few good sized patches I stopped to re-group and we waited for some time. After a bit longer, I went back to see that our high country expert had knocked himself out totally. He'd previously ignored what I'd said and had been blasting through the smaller bulldust holes at speed until he met this one that had the hidden edges that I tried to explain and it bought him to grief.

The bike had been partly submerged in the hole and high-country had hit the exit wall of the hole at speed. It launched him over the handlebars and knocked him out cold. He'd gotten away with the earlier ones, hadn't heard my briefing because he was an expert and his lack of experience in this area had given him a false sense of security and he simply didn't see the trap coming.

Alternatively, we have the guy who was talked into doing a Cape York trip by his mates. He's normally a capable rider but he has succumbed to peer pressure and he is so out of his depth and paranoid and overly cautious that he lets the water truck overtake him at 40 kilometres per hour on a good gravel highway. Yes, that's right, the oversized water carrying trucks with a series of spray nozzles used for dust control around road maintenance sites.

I don't want to be pointing fingers here or putting anybody down. The build-up and excitement of the trip throws them out of their depth, and being so eager to just get going sends them into a first day fever and beyond. This is not about one singular person but a roll over copy of what I've seen 1000 times. I'm all about being inclusive and showing every single person a great time and every one of these riders have actually all had an awesome adventure riding experience. I'm just trying to say BE HONEST with yourself and don't go looking for your limits and boundaries. Be calm, walk before you run and think before you act. Adventure riding usually includes multiple days of getting to know your bike and the area you are riding in. Pace yourself and enjoy each day – learn the terrain, train your eyes to see it and you will enjoy a deeper connection with the places you are riding in.

Don't be in a rush to have a good time!

CHAPTER 3

The people you meet

There are so many places to see and ride – I've been lucky to travel all over Australia and my job has opened up so many opportunities that would have never come my way without the people that I've met. Like I said in the introduction the adventure is more than half made by the people. I've had the opportunity to travel to the USA and through Thailand and all because of people I met in Cape York.

Alaska to Mexico

I flew to America over four legs that took 27 hours and while I was waiting in Seattle to get on my last flight to Anchorage the flight was cancelled three times so I got to know my bar buddy pretty well. He lived in Anchorage and offered me a place to stay while I got myself organised for the upcoming adventure. I had been sent to the USA to ride from Alaska to Mexico over seven weeks. It was a reconnaissance mission to seek out the best trails with iconic scenes and travel locations for a group of wealthy businessmen who wanted to ride this trek in sections the following year.

Upon my arrival to my new buddy's house he couldn't wait to show me his gun collection, which I was soon to find out was fairly commonplace in this part of the world. He showed me all around Anchorage and took me to the bike dealer. I purchased one of the first dual-sport Triumph Tigers with a pretty heavy case of jet-lag to find out that I had a tight deadline to get out of dodge. The dealer was a top guy and helped me out heaps and informed me that the first snows were on their way and if I didn't get out of there in the next day or so I was going to be stuck in Alaska for three months. It didn't give me as much time to customise the brand new bike and get my gear sorted in the panniers as I would have liked but I figured I could work it out as I went. I'm not used to that sort of cold so it was a no-brainer to get out and get going.

I got my route planned and headed into Denali National Park. Alaska to me is the Cape York of the Americas, it was as wild and as beautiful as I had imagined it to be. When you see the television shows with the moose and elk walking down the street and the salmon-filled rivers, it's not a movie set – it is real life. The scenery is absolutely astounding, the blue of the mountains spearing into the sky with their white tipped arrows and the grass as green as I've ever seen.

Dawson Creek in British Columbia is the southernmost boundary of the Alaska Highway and for this reason it is sometimes called "Mile 0 City". It was a pretty popular television show that came out that year, apparently – I knew this because Renae was excited that I'd been there. I headed down the Alaskan highway that was just a dirt road at the time I travelled it and found myself overtaking big campervans and RV's that had moose horns and elk antlers hanging all over them. The hunters were all heading home before winter set it in. I met a few in the roadhouses and they all told me what a great season they'd had. They've all got permits and they have a yearly hunt allowance. I thought that was a great system that would probably work well to manage our growing crocodile population.

The Alaskan highway reminded me of Australia with its vast open plains for hundreds of kilometres but then I'd come across soaring snow-clad mountains and I'd remember where I was. The log cabin houses dotted the landscape and they had a coating of grass on the roof for insulation that I'd never seen before. It was a totally different experience for me and I couldn't wait to see what was around the next corner. I just remember it being the place where all the boys had lots of very big toys like snowmobiles and airplanes and gun lockers to go hunting for bears.

Whitehorse is a town straight out of a western movie in Canada's Yukon Territory, where the rivers transform into lakes and the temperature regularly drops to -40c, not that I experienced that. I was lucky to be in a prolonged summer and I managed to avoid those temperatures and had the ideal conditions for my route south. My itinerary was planned to avoid any major cities and seek out the finest tourist destinations and I headed into Alberta, Canada next. Banff National Park and Lake Louise were beyond my belief, with rows of maple and pine trees and where the sheer granite cliffs fell into pools of the bluest of blue water you've ever seen. It's an absolute picture perfect postcard and you couldn't make it any more spectacular or beautiful if you tried.

I'm a keen golfer so I stayed in Banff and played a round of golf at the Banff Springs Hotel Golf Course. The pro shop paired me up with a fella who was visiting from Palm Springs, California. There were herds of elk that inhabited different parts of the golf course and I'd never witnessed anything like this in my life. So I hit a shot and my ball landed right near a big bull. I kind of figured that this was a well-used course and that they shouldn't hurt me so I attempted to play on. Well instinct is stronger than I thought so when that bull showed me his antlers and started to charge, I shat myself and thought I was going to be impaled on those horns. I ran straight to the golf cart and floored it to as fast as it would go, which isn't fast enough. I took note that the elk bull followed and seemed to maintain the same speed as me and then I noted my mate laughing his head off. He explained that it's just a display not a threat, he's just making sure you know that these are his girls, he wasn't going to gore you. So, elk will charge but then stop at a safe distance away, good to know! Also good to know that I wasn't the first person he'd seen do the dash. He gave me his contact details to catch up with him when I was in his area.

In Wyoming I visited Yellowstone National Park, which features dramatic canyons, alpine rivers, lush forests, hot springs and gushing geysers, including the famous Old Faithful. I was unfortunate to come through after a bushfire the year before so the whole place was charred and recovering but I still found it pretty special with the geysers, and the herds and herds of bison.

THE PEOPLE YOU MEET

I stayed in Jackson which is a snow skiing town full of resorts on the border of Yellowstone. This is where I discovered that every little town had its own micro-brewery and you could have any type of beer that you wanted. It was a new experience for me and I'm happy to see it taking place in Australia these days. Yes, all the bar stools were topped with saddles.

When you see the Redwood Forest in California for the first time it's just like walking into the land of the giants. There were several trees that had hollows in their bases that were big enough to drive a car through. I rode over the Golden Gate in San Francisco and went on to stay with friends in Los Angeles. Well, actually it was a father and son team that had done the Cape Tour the year before and I hung out with them for a couple of days' recovery. I met up with my golfing buddy in Palm Springs and we played on one of the many lush green golf courses that are surrounded by stark red desert. Palm Springs is really something to see.

I emptied my wallet playing Blackjack in Las Vegas, Nevada! Not because I play badly mind you. There was this waitress who couldn't seem to stop serving me. I was really impressed with the service at the beginning of the night but after a few hours I wondered if she had a crush on me or thought that I was Robert DeNiro or something. I couldn't put an empty glass down. She was right there ready to serve every time. I did think the drinks were a bit expensive though and I gave her a $10 chip each time. It wasn't until the next day that I found out that the drinks were free at the casino tables and I'd been handing out really big tips all night.

Speaking of that Robert DeNiro look alike thing; I stayed in Tucson and was out looking for a place to eat, probably looking like a tourist. People were looking at me weirdly and doing double takes, one even took a picture which creeped me out so I decided to move on, when I saw the huge 'Ronin the Movie' poster splashed up on the wall behind me. Type Ronin the Movie into Google, do you think it looks like me?

I caught up with my bosses in El Paso, Texas. We'd planned to meet and do a five-day tour in Copper Canyon. That was an interesting ride, it was very similar to the videos you see on the Himalayas – tight winding trails with sheer drops into never-never land below. The company hired bikes that were well suited to the trails they were doing like DR's and KLX's dirt bikes and our Mexican tour guide was a bit concerned about taking me on the Triumph Tiger. The trails were pretty hair-raising and with the rocky bumps and humps they were really more suited for goats, but I'd been on the big girl so long we were used to each other and got through it pretty good I reckon. We arrived at a t-intersection and our guide looked really confused as to whether we should go right or left so I asked him where we had to get to that night. I was fortunate enough to have the latest and greatest GPS technology on my bike and was able to lead the group in to our overnight stay.

It was a real saviour on that trip and I would never had made it through the 7000 miles without it. I left my bike with the father and son to sell and I flew back home from Los Angeles with a couple of pairs of roller blades for my kids.

Thailand

I met up with a German fella at one of the resorts on our tour route. He was very interested in what we did and made a beeline for us as soon as he saw us rock up. He asked me a heap of questions and I found out later that he did a similar tour in Thailand. After a long chat that night we kept in touch while he was travelling around the area for quite a few weeks, and he stayed with us for a few nights before flying back to Germany. At that time he invited me to join him on one of his next tours. This was back in the early 90's before Thailand was even being talked about in Australia so I was very keen to get involved. It was also at the beginning of our business venture so I was interested to see how they did it in other parts of the world and get some pointers.

THE PEOPLE YOU MEET

I took him up on the offer and flew to Bangkok. From there I caught a bus to meet with my mate in Chiang Mai in the northern part of Thailand. I remember being on this fully-laden double-decker bus and I was pretty sure the driver was half cut because he'd just pull out on an open stretch of highway for no reason and the people coming head on in the opposite direction just had to find a way to get around him. I couldn't believe this traffic and the sheer amount of it. That was a real eye-opener, and the amount of bikes on the roads really surprised me all in one tiny place. It established the thought for me that Australia was such a small percentage of the market and that we are insignificant in the global motorcycle marketplace.

I was introduced to the other riders in the group, all German, and with myself made up our group of twelve riders. I met the support driver, who was in a Suzuki Sierra to transport luggage only. We were to be accommodated and catered for the entire journey.

The terrain was very similar to the Daintree – red clay, lush rainforests and very hilly and very much what I was comfortable riding being just like home. The bikes weren't real good and a mixed bag of DR250's, XR250's and DT175's. They all had plenty of miles on them but there wasn't much option given that they couldn't get anything over 150cc in Thailand at the time. These had all been sourced from the black market in Japan and shipped over in containers. I got given a Suzuki DR250 and it felt like I was riding a wet sponge, everything just sagged. Nonetheless it was about the experience and the culture and the people.

It was awesome going from village to village every 20 kilometres or so. The people were so very friendly and it was super exciting for them to see these big bikes and they would crowd around us like we were rock stars. I was particularly blown away by the long neck tribe. Each year or so the ladies would add a new ring to their necklace and some ladies were sporting an adornment that was as tall as a ruler between their head and shoulders. That was really something to see. Each village seemed to have a different culture and a different dialect. We went into Burma where even on the smallest trail there were soldiers with machine guns that would hold your passport to ensure that you would return and depart the county.

On the second last night of the ride I was sitting and chatting with my mate over dinner. He was planning out the next day's ride, it was going to be an issue with wet weather coming in and I was told that the route was going to be very hilly and slippery when wet. After being with the group for a few days I had a better idea of their capabilities and suggested that we make an alteration to a better suited route for this group but he insisted that it would be fine, Fräulein. Sure enough it rained through the night and into the next morning. We embarked on the trail and the group spread out and slowly dropped out across several different villages. The group dwindled down to just three riders and these guys had reported the message up to me out front. We were now 50 kilometres ahead of the next rider who had called it quits.

With very little English between us we decided to stay at the village that we were in. It was a shanty town community village with no shops or hotels or anything. The locals were very hospitable and offered food and beds for the night. They started cooking us up some tucker for an afternoon snack that looked a lot like goat balls and I really think they were. The bedding on offer was as inviting as the goat balls and I opted to take my chances to make it into Chiang Mai. It was only a couple of hundred clicks away and the appeal of a luxury hotel bed, satisfying meal and a beer in the bar had me won over. They stayed and I took off on a mission.

I couldn't speak any Thai so the only option I had for directions was to pull up to the first person I saw in each of the villages and say, "Chiang Mai?". The villagers obliged and pointed me in that direction. I could eventually see the lights of the big city in the distance from the hills and I followed the roads that I thought would lead me toward them. I was in flight zone on my wet sponge and having a great time slipping and *sliding into the trails just like at home. It ended up being an awesome, adventure-packed day and a better evening in my soft white sheets with a full tummy and wondering if the boys ate those goat balls. I met up with the group the following day and we all had a quiet dinner together before I flew home.*

There's something about a motorcycle that makes people incredibly generous and welcoming. I've been so fortunate to meet some fantastic people that I still consider mates to this day.

CHAPTER 4

Take yourself

The station owner

When I was travelling around the Kimberley region of Western Australia 35 years ago, I was with a schoolteacher at the time and we had teamed up to do the Gibb River Road. It was getting late in the day and we were thinking we'd better find somewhere to camp for the night when we came across a station homestead. We went up to the door and asked the farmer if he minded if we camped on his property for the night. He was your typical cattle station owner with one leg of his jeans rolled up to the knee, chewing on a stalk of grass while I was having a chat with him. The farmer was pretty welcoming and had absolutely no problem telling us about an old gorge that was just down the way about five kilometres from the homestead. I think he was grateful to have someone new to talk to. So after a real long chat we headed off following his directions.

Sure enough we found the old gorge and we were absolutely blown away. It was jaw-droppingly beautiful and worthy of a Hollywood movie set. In the late afternoon sun, the harsh redness of the outback rock escarpments was softened blue by the water reflections, and there was a scattering of green from the few Boab trees that were throwing eerie shadows on the walls.

The teacher and I set up our swags and camp as quick as we could and I emptied out my gear looking for my fishing kit. There was an old boat sitting on the edge of the water and being a keen fisherman, I really wanted to catch a fish. The boat had obviously been dragged over the rocks and the bottom was badly pitted with holes everywhere, so we taped it up with good ole gaffer tape and paddled down the gorge. As soon as the line hit the water we were catching barra[5], after barra, after barra, all the way until we reached the end of the canyon. I felt pretty small and insignificant in the valley and it was like going to church when I discovered the Quinkan rock art on the red stone walls. I've seen a few Aboriginal paintings since but this one is in my mind as the biggest and most beautiful that I have ever seen. It was a truly magnificent and ancient landscape and I was in heaven.

The sunset was as spectacular as the red earth it was reflecting and I noted that the kookaburras here laughed differently to the ones down south. We had a good feed of the barramundi that evening and slept so well with the campfire crackling and the waterfall sounds lulling us into a deep slumber. This is five million-star accommodation I thought.

The following day we sadly departed. I wanted to thank the farmer for his hospitality and all I had to give was a couple of fish I'd caught. I was thinking to myself the whole way to the homestead that he was probably sick of barra but I delivered them anyway. Can you believe he was shocked and said, "Where did you get them from?". UM, well we went to the gorge that you gave us the directions to yesterday afternoon. It turns out that he'd never been to the gorge, he was dumbfounded by my explanations and was shocked to hear what he had on his property!

---

[5] Barra – Barramundi, a prized fish to catch.

TAKE YOURSELF

Mind you the station was only 700,000 acres. This is what adventure riding is all about, in the middle of nowhere you will find incredible hidden gems!

Depending on where you live it can be pretty hard to find adventures just around the corner that are exciting to ride and legal. You're going to have to take yourself out there. Don't ride in areas where you know you're not allowed to be. Always have permission or you're going to piss off the owners, land managers or anyone who lives close and that's what gets tracks closed for us all. Be mindful to uphold a good reputation for all trail bike riders that are going to follow along behind you. We are so lucky in Australia to have such an enormous amount of diversity and the freedom to choose what we want to see. You can start your journey from any point and visit such amazing locations along the way. It was my choice to do all of the famous outback Australian stock routes because I had had the vision to do the motorcycle tours in Cape York and before I committed to that destination I wanted to make sure that I had made the correct choice. I wanted to end up in a place that had all the variety of riding that I craved and so I set about eliminating any doubts and ticking them all off to confirm that Cape York was in fact the most diverse adventure riding and the last frontier in Australia, to me.

I don't want to sound biased here, but I am…Cape York was the number one choice because it contained all of my desires that I had been dreaming about since I was a kid. Having said that, I can only say that because I have actually done them all and so should you! Go on, take yourself and find your fantasy adventure destination. It is out there.

Once you've selected your adventure destination it's time to do your research and prepare yourself on the best way to achieve it. Buy topographical maps, watch documentaries, do your research on Google and ask about other people's experiences, information is easy to find these days. Ask me, I'm always happy to talk about adventure riding. Get to know your area before you go.

In Central Australia you'll find countless famous, iconic tracks that include; the Simpson Desert; the Birdsville Track; the Plenty Highway; the Oodnadatta track; and the Gun Barrel Highway, just to name a few. These tracks are made up of predominantly sand and bulldust. When you're out on these trails you can look across the horizon and see the curvature of the earth and nothing else. It's true Australian outback and red as far as the eye can see. The landscape is made up of a high percentage of iron oxide so it is actually rust. The rusty old outback! You'll be lucky to see a tree, only the toughest of species can survive and you can travel for a whole day and not see another person. As long as you have prepared well it's pretty safe to travel out here solo as there are plenty of townships and fuel stops since it has become more popular.

TAKE YOURSELF

Which reminds me about this little Japanese fella I met while I was roaming around the Oodnadatta track. Now the Oodnadatta Track is 620 kilometres of remote outback gravel road that goes from Maree to Marla in South Australia. We'd both stopped in Oodnadatta itself to camp for the night and it's always good to have a chat with a fellow adventure rider. He couldn't speak much English but we shared the bikes in common and struck up a conversation of mostly sign language. So we sat around the camp and pointed at things for a while and agreed that we could understand each other, when he pulls out a map. He pointed to where we were. I agreed nodding, yes we are at Oodnadatta on the Oodnadatta Track, "Yep". Then he pointed to Melbourne on the map and said, "Tomorrow". Now I wasn't sure at this point if he really meant tomorrow or if he thought that word meant something else. I looked at him pretty surprised that he wanted to achieve some 1500 kilometre journey in a day. He'd have to start now and not stop riding for the next 20 hours. I shook my head and answered with a, "No". I found myself thinking later that he might have flown in here somehow because why else would he think he could do that span of the map in a day, if he'd ridden here from that map in the first place.

The western region will give you; the Kimberley's Gibb River Road and the Canning Stock Route which are the most famous and iconic trails in the west. The Canning Stock Route was once regarded as one of the loneliest and most difficult routes to conquer because it was around 2000 kilometres of desert, traversing the Great Sandy Desert, the Little Sandy Desert and the Gibson Desert. It has got some stories to tell if you're into history and it's extreme. You'd have to take everything you need to be self-sufficient in this area and it requires a whole other level of planning – don't do it alone!!!

High country hills in Victoria and on the New South Wales border is where I grew up riding. It's so very different to what we do now. This is a pretty special place where the trails wind up, down and over the mountain ranges. On the peaks it's not uncommon to ride through a cloud formation that's very similar to fog, some don't even recognise that it's an actual cloud they're riding in. The single tracks are spectacular with greenery, the trees are tall and dotted with ferns and mossy fallen logs. The hills drop off forever and sometimes it's so bloody cold that you can't even pull the clutch. We didn't have anything like heated grips back then so when our fingers froze solid we used to pull over and grab the exhaust pipe just to get some feeling back. The old Belstaff jackets were more like an oiled Drizabone than the jackets are now and they weren't so good at keeping the chill out. So I spent a fair bit of money on The Age and The Herald newspapers, not to catch up on the news but to wrap my body before I put my jacket on. I'm not really built for the cold.

So let's head up north to the sun and Tropical North Queensland's, Cape York – ah that's better. Cape York has the diversity of Australia all in one location. I always say that it has every Australian terrain type except snow. Perfect! Cape York offers desert outback trails, world heritage rainforests and is unmatched with its innumerable water networks with little streams, crystal clear creeks and major rivers to negotiate so frequently. I think that's what makes it so special. The landscapes are like dominoes placed between the water networks – you can be in thick muddy rainforest in the morning, cross a stream into sparse savannah lands, cross a river and find yourself on an outback desert trail. Every day has a surprising change.

The Old Telegraph track is the iconic track up here made up of mostly narrow sections that are very rocky and eroded, it's definitely 4WD only. The original track was created in the 1880s to connect Cairns with Thursday Island. So we were there with a tour group and I was feeling a bit cheeky. Every morning we do a daily briefing and I instructed all the boys on what to expect for the day. I was explaining that these crystal-clear creeks are deceiving and the depth cannot be known by vision alone, and that we would have to walk across to check the depth. Don't take for granted that you can see the bottom clearly as it looks one foot deep but is probably more like four foot. So I instructed them to take these precautions throughout the day and if it was too deep I would be there to show them the correct line to take.

I was out front with a bit of time to spare at the first creek so I waited until I could hear the next rider coming. I rushed the crossing when I made eye contact with the rider coming around the corner, followed by the next rider and the next. They all saw me chest deep in the water with only the mirror in view above the waterline. They were all gawking at me, horrified and wondering what the hell had gone wrong here with our guide cocking it up so badly. Holding on and struggling with "my bike under the water", I urgently pointed with one hand for them to take the rocky edge all the way around this thoroughfare, go downstream where it's shallower and then come all the way back around and up to the trail over there, which I pointed out. That was the best line to take. They all obligingly followed my instruction. They kept throwing concerned peeks at me as they struggled a little bit with the new route but they continued on. When they all safely got to the other side…I got up off my knees with my mirror in my hand and walked over to them. They were all laughing at me then and calling me a few choice names but they didn't take these creeks for granted and no one drowned a bike for the rest of the trip. But on a serious note these creeks and streams are usually deeper than they look.

The CREB (Cairns Regional Electricity Board) track is a super special track, it's one of my all-time favourites because it's just like a box of chocolates; you never know which one you're gonna get, thanks Forrest Gump. This track goes through the heart of the World Heritage Daintree Rainforest and snakes and weaves its way through a sequence of creeks, hills and mountains and it is seriously fun and seriously deceiving. You can come in at one end of the track and it will be dry but as you rise up through the trail you can find yourself in a rain storm. If it's wet you're going to be in a whole other movie. The red clay becomes super slick and requires every single skill you have to negotiate the steep uphills and the ever-falling downhills that end straight into a switchback corner. At some times of year it's almost impossible to walk and can become impassable to vehicles. We have been caught out many times and being that it is the first day of our tour in most cases, it can be quite the rude awakening for the group. If the track misbehaves the whole group is forced into a survival scenario and at the time they feel like it's life and death but in reality it's only a bed they're gonna miss out on. We work as a team to get through these tests and it becomes the most exhilarating thing they've ever done. Now I don't want to scare you off here, I highly recommend this track to any rider – just be careful to do it in the dry and watch the weather.

If you come through here at the end of the wet season and before the traffic starts you will come across some fresh growths of the infamous 'wait-a-while' vine. Now you have to know about this vindictive little vine if you want to travel in this area because it is nature's barbed wire and every stem has hooked teeth that grab onto you, which seems pretty tame, right up until you try to get out of it. Then you register its name, 'wait-a-while', as it clings and bites in tightening its hold. Being that I ride out front this nightmare of a plant has certainly taken its pound of flesh from me and mostly off my poor snoz that's exposed between the mouth guard of my helmet and my goggles.

Then there are the fallen trees that appear around the switchback corner halfway up a slimy red hill, that's a tonne of fun. It really gets the heart pumping. Then you realise the tree trunk is a metre tall off the ground and you just simply have no other route around it on this hill. What now, do we turn back? No, we never turn back I think. The answer is here, we just have to think about it. There's no traction on this greasy surface and I'm certainly not going to pop the front wheel that high. So we need a launch ramp and I start cutting the branches off the tree. I've learnt to pack a trusty sharp toothed blade into my back pack at the beginning of the season because you just never know what has happened to the trails after the wet.

So with all these hassles that lay ahead of us – why do we keep doing it? Because, for most of us, it's genetic and just plain hard-wired into our brains to seek adventure and the sensations that stimulate the survival instinct, according to Professor Marvin Zuckerman. I feel that is certainly true of me, I crave those bodily vibrations that make me think about how I can and will survive this hiccup. Oddly, that's when I feel most alive.

*We had a group of high-powered businessmen come on tour with us that had an article published in a weekly business magazine. The journalist interviewed the riders and the mutual comments rounded out like this, "The trip was about adventure, comradery and being silly… and that boys need to get dirty sometimes". If you have a demanding job you need to find a balance of work, family and things that interest you. If you are constantly thinking about work, can't escape the phone and the thoughts of business replay in your head, just remember that these guys said what they enjoyed most about their adventure was that **the physical exertion joined with a perception of survival is mentally relaxing.** No matter who you are, you won't be thinking about work when you're concentrating on getting your bike through the mud and sand or a river crossing. It's OK to take time off and enjoy your life. An adventure will do you a world of good and help you to re-assess your life for the better.*

On the flip side of this there can be some seriously sad reasons to take on an adventure ride. I had the pleasure of meeting a petite female rider, Ann, who was an inspirational powerhouse. She came on tour with her son and she was very green on the off-road sections. Don't get me wrong at all here, Ann was brave and determined, she was going to make it to the top come hell or high water and with that determination the guides and I were so willing to help her every step of the way. I just love seeing that 'grit' in people and it means I'm gonna work so much harder to make her dream a reality.

After a few days, I knew Ann was working solidly and must have been exhausted and I was curious as to why she was doing this and so I asked. She told me that it had been a bucket-list item for her late husband who had suffered with depression and committed suicide a few years earlier. Being the amazing person that she is and with two teenage children to raise on her own, Ann decided to look life in the eyes and follow through with every single adventure that was on that list. They skydived, bushwalked and rafted – you name it.

Cape York was last to be ticked off as her son had to grow up and get his license and she had to learn to ride a bike. The day Ann stood on the tip[6], holding the iconic sign and capturing the moment on film, was overwhelming for every single person on that tour. She smiled, she cried, she hugged her boy, she laughed and cried some more! The emotions were on overload for everyone. We were all so bloody proud of her and humbly honoured to be a part of her epic moment.

We've done quite a few memorial rides and been witness to ashes being spread for a lost father or friend and watched the changes in people as they shed the sadness in the world and grow in a shared adventure. It truly is amazing to observe but for all the sadness that can occur it is equally met with joy and cheerful occasions. I even got to be best man at a wedding at the highest beach in Cape York once. The bride and groom rode from Cairns to Cape York with their wedding attire and favourite champagne in their bags. The bride wore boots under her wedding dress and they rode their Honda CRF's to the ceremony.

We've just touched the surface of the places you can go and the things you might find. There are so many spaces to explore on this

---

[6] The Tip – The northernmost point of the Australian Continent.

planet and so many reasons why you should do it. Everything is achievable with a bit of proper preparation and creative ingenuity to get you through.

CHAPTER 5

Traps for young players

So there I was on my trip around Australia out in the middle of nowhere, when lo and behold I came across this massive salt pan. I couldn't believe my eyes, "How good is this, my very own Bonneville". Any motorcyclist worth his salt will have the same first thought, "How much fun would that be?". Next minute I was off to have some fun cutting loose with some big skids, opposite locks and having the time of my life. It was hard and fast while I was on the gas but a lake of quicksand the minute I wasn't!!! Before I knew it the boat sunk and I was axel deep in black sludge. I attempted to use the motor to help me push the bike out but only managed to dig myself deeper into the sludge. Every time I attempted to pull the bike out I ended up knee deep and it was hard work to pull myself out. Then it occurred to me that I was out in the middle of this salt pan in 40-degree heat. I was looking around at the moonscape before me and there was nothing, nothing I could use to lever the bike out. There was not a tree in sight to offer any shade, I had a limited supply of water and nobody was coming *along to help me any time soon. The only thing I could think of to help me get out of this predicament was to lay the bike on its side and get it out of the suction hold that was gripping it like a vice. Then I took the sheepskin seat cover off my bike and laid it on the ground to stand on. I needed to get some purchase without sinking and enough of it so I could flip the bike over. Wash, rinse, repeat, flip, over and over again until I eventually got it back onto solid ground. So that's what I did for the next four hours; side-to-side roll overs and cartwheeled the bloody thing out of there. I rode away looking like a lamington, rolled in mud and dusted with salt going from hero to zero in two minutes flat.*

Dust

If you've ever been on tour with me you will know that I am like a broken record when it comes to the warnings about dust. I say it a thousand times, "Don't ride in the dust!". All too often it's human nature to want to keep up with the rider out front. Or if you're trying to overtake a vehicle there seems to be this build-up of urgency that comes about that lulls the rider into taking the risk and heading out into the blinding cloud of dust billowing out from behind the vehicle. Not only is this life-threatening and could be fatal, it's not good for your health or the health of the motorcycle. Be patient and take your time to make these judgement calls, staying out of the dust will give you a longer visibility to be able to make a safe decision. Staying out of the dust will also protect the bike because it won't be sucking all that dust into the air filter. The knock-on effect is a longer lifespan for your motor and yourself.

Riding alongside

If you're riding out with mates and you want to pair up to ride side-by-side make the decision in advance as to who is going to drop back when you come into a corner or meet a vehicle coming in the opposite direction. I've seen it many time where you both shut off at the same time and the rider on the outside gets blocked out in the danger zone. My rule here is that the rider on the inside remains constant and the rider on the outside is the one who should alternate. The rider on the outside should be the more experienced rider and positioned slightly back off the front riders wheel when on the outside. This is a simple little tip that will save lives.

Bulldust

Bulldust is a totally different sensation from sand, it's a pool of talcum powder that doesn't have any body or substance to it and it's almost like water and a ghost that appears out of nowhere. It can hide boulders, washouts and the sharp edged walls that contain it. You have to train your eyes to look for it. Once it's experienced for the first time it won't be soon forgotten, if you make it through unscathed. Usually bulldust will be dust red or dirt white depending on the area that you're riding in. You need to test the waters before you charge in, just like any water crossing. This is one of the biggest traps that we have in outback Australia.

One thing I regularly tell my riders is that if you see an obstacle such as big pools of dust, sand, deep ruts, dry obstacles that are likely to catch you out, or something that is just plain daunting – take a look around you for an easier line. This rule doesn't apply to wet sections and mud holes. Water will pool in sections of the road or trail but the base will be firm, if you try to go around a mud hole it is likely that you will end up in a softer section than the one you were on.

Don't be pressured to stay on the road if it looks dangerous or makes you nervous. We can go off-road or off-trail. As simple as this sounds a lot of people will automatically just stick to the path that lays in front of them. The brain works in mysterious ways doesn't it? That simple change will make a whole lot of difference to your ride. If you can't get off the road and around it for whatever reason then take a moment to consider what the best and safest line might be. Don't just charge in but check for the best and safest route. Once you choose, commit to it and look forward, as far forward as is required. Only look at the line you have chosen – this play on visualisation works! Where you look is where you will go, magically the bike just follows.

Slick

One of the things that you can expect to see in the high country and need to be very careful of is wet and icy surfaces. For instance, timber bridges.

A long time ago one of these slick traps caught me out big time. You just can't see how slippery it is until you actually hit it. As an inexperienced rider coming into this situation for the first time I hit that bridge at a rapid speed and before I could blink, the front wheel immediately disappeared from under me. I had no time to react and body-slammed hard, my head and shoulders hit the deck first. I was knocked out cold for a good 10-15 minutes and I woke up to my riding companions sitting me up on the side of the trail taking my helmet off. They told me later that I was asking them repeatedly; "Where are we? What are we doing?" Apparently I was fit enough to ride my bike back to the carpark because that's where I really woke up. As soon as I saw my vehicle with a bike trailer on it my memory jolted back fully. I learned a big lesson that day – if the ground is wet or shiny it usually means 'slippery' and to tread with caution.

Animals

These largely come in one of two categories – animals and vegetables (drivers in/on other vehicles) – and are equally sudden and unpredictable and you have to stay focused. Pigs, cows and kangaroos are common hazards in Cape York and they can pop up anywhere, anytime. There are two pointers you can consider to reduce your chances of a collision. Firstly they will be most active around dawn and dusk, so slow down when riding at these times, and keep an eye on both sides of your trail.

Speaking about wildlife, this one sure came as a surprise to me. I was leading a tour group on a remote beach in Cape York. It was a coastal section with numerous rocky outcrops reaching out into the water with small bays of beaches dotted along the route. It's one of my favourite rides and just has everything you could wish for in a beach ride: World War II wrecks; awesome fishing; big black lipped oysters on the rocks and the list goes on. If for some reason you get stranded out here you can live like a KING. I just love this place and often take my friends out there for our holidays.

So I was negotiating one of the rocky outcrops that had been eroded by the waves over time, creating stepped ledges like a staircase with different sized steps. If you pick your line well you can ride one of these ledges around the point and stay out of the salt water surf. As I rounded the point something caught my eye and started moving along the rock ledge towards me at the speed of light. "Holy shit," I thought. "It's a bloody crocodile." He must have been sunbathing on the warmed rock bed. He hadn't heard me coming around the corner with the wind blowing in the opposite direction. He was making his way to the protection of the water and I was making my way to the beach bay and neither of us were willing to give up that rock ledge. In hindsight I probably would have without question had I had the time to think about it. I was committed and we were going to cross paths. As he came wiggling toward me like a bullet I had no option but to hit his back, clutch it and pop the wheel up. He turned on me like a snake, snapping and swinging his jaws in a pretty pissed off manner. He made it very clear that he wasn't impressed and would take a chunk out of both me and the bike if I didn't disappear right now.

As quick as he came at me he straightened up and shot into the waves. By the time my front tyre made ground fall he was gone. This all happened in the blink of an eye and I rode away about 100 metres to what I thought was a safe distance, heart pumping loudly in my chest, and turned to the rider following behind me. I yelled out to him, "Did you see that?". He said, "HUH!". Bloody hell, not one witness on the planet, much to my disappointment. The croc would have been at least three metres and it took a while for it to become clear in my head that I had just done a wheelie over a croc!

TRAPS FOR YOUNG PLAYERS

You've really got to be careful of all sorts of animals and there are a few tips that will help you predict where they might be. The second pointer comes when approaching any waterways, dips or cattle grids – beware! They will graze or take shelter from the heat in the low lying areas where water may pool, this is where the trees will grow and create shade and the grass gets greener. Be aware of the lay of the land and travel cautiously. Even if you can't see anything you should always expect some kind of animal to be in any dip in the road. This has saved me hundreds of times over the years.

This lesson was learned the hard way; I was riding on a good gravel road one day cruising at a good pace. The outback cattle country roads are dotted with dips and cattle grates that you have to be cautious about and this day as I approached a dip a cow appeared out of the tall guinea grass alongside the road. She started running, bucking and farting along the road and heading in the same direction as me. I slammed on my front and rear brake, trying to avoid the inevitable collision and I was all locked up sliding toward this beast. I knew I was gone and that this was really going to hurt. I braced for impact because she couldn't outrun the pace that I was at and there was no stopping this mess. We collided, my bike hitting the rear end of the cow and I'd lost all control. I found myself laying on the cow's big ass and as it felt me land she kicked up big time and bucked me right back onto my bike. The pressure of my landing back into the seat forced the bike to correct itself. NO BULLSHIT! I rode away unscathed heading in the same direction.

Second time around; I was doing a reconnaissance ride for the BMW Safari across the gulf country when I came across a similar situation again. The road was good and I could see greenery in the dry dip, so even though there was no water I knew from the above experience not to trust the quiet look of the scene ahead. As cautious as I was I still got caught out by a kangaroo jumping out in front of me and I just couldn't avoid him. Luckily I was on a big bike that had some substantial weight behind it to take some of the impact – had I been on a smaller bike I would have been on the ground.

These are the types of things that you need to look out for when you come to any dips in the road. Even if you don't necessarily see water, in the greenery or shade is where the wildlife will be. Another good pointer is to remember that animals usually don't hang out alone so if you see one, brake hard and look for the other that could be coming from any direction.

Vegetables[7]

Never assume that you, or the group, are the only ones using the tracks and trails because even in the most isolated places you will encounter other vehicles. Common sense and the road rules say keep left, especially on blind corners. Don't float out wide and don't go faster than your vision because chances are high that the person driving in the opposite direction may not be as sensible as

---

[7] Vegetables – The driver or rider who is not paying attention.

you, and could very well be taking up more than their fair share of the track. Crests are another danger so get up on the pegs for a quick check before reaching the top. One of my favourite sayings is, "Expect the unexpected", and for all of its meanings, one is to trust no one. It's really important that you don't assume that other road users can see you. I've looked a driver straight in the eyes and watched him pull out in front of me. Riding a motorcycle is like wearing an invisibility cloak so drive that way.

Ruts

There are two problematic ruts, on an adventure ride, that are caused by 4WD's; the first is where the 4WD wheel tracks leave a rut that remains soft and sandy. The other more common will be caused by 4WD's that have gone through the mud and left their tyre impressions for the sun to bake it hard into the trail, like train tracks. They can appear on an open road or in tighter sections where you wouldn't expect a vehicle to have been. If they are deep and ominous – look to go around it. The biggest problem I see people having is when they charge into the rut at speed and the front wheel catches the edge. The bike reacts like it's on rails and the rider tries madly to get out of it, gets all crossed up and over they go. If you see ruts and you have to ride through them make sure you slow down to an appropriate speed, look at the rut you are in – not the one next to it – and keep a constant throttle, and the bike should cruise through.

If you find yourself in the situation where the front tyre has grabbed the edge most people will respond by rolling off the throttle and this is what gets you out of shape. You have to train your mind to power on or even accelerate to get that tyre free-flowing again. I know it's difficult to do when your fear response kicks in and screams at you to go slower but if you ever get into this situation try it and you will see that it will pull you out. This is especially true in sandy ruts.

The other type of rut is caused by water damage and erosion. Clean roads with no tracks are a sure sign of booby traps ahead for me. Fresh out of the wet season in the Cape when we are one of the first to be riding on the roads and trails, I always feel a bit on edge if I can't see any tyre marks ahead of me. Don't get me wrong that's the best time to be there BUT there are hidden traps. You can be riding along and see the road for miles and miles ahead into the distance and then all of a sudden you're up on a two metre crevice that was almost invisible. Washouts form where a previously ankle deep trickle has turned into a raging creek foaming with whitewash and munching up the road that it's making its way across. The problem is that water cuts clean, creating sharp-edged walls on either side and exposing the rock and boulders on the bottom. The image of the road ahead merges, hiding the washout and you just can't see it. You have no idea how wide it is or how deep it is until you're upon it. Dips that have been concrete-lined, like a causeway, end up with the edges of the concrete being exposed and this creates a major hazard. Be aware of the season you're riding in and what may have happened after any weather event.

These dips can lull a rider into a false sense of security too, they are numerous in our area and most of them are pretty minor blips in the journey but they are inconsistent so don't be fooled into thinking that this one is going to be the same as the last ten you just went through.

These dips can hide a B-Double on the wrong side of the road trying to find his best line out of his situation. Now I know these roads like the back of my hand and on one occasion I was riding with a group of friends having a great time speeding into the dip and gaining airtime on the way out over and over again until I came up to one that had a 4WD on my side of the road. Old mate was stopped in the bottom leaning back and telling the kids to be quiet. I had nowhere to go but into his vehicle. Luckily I managed to avoid the bulbar but clipped the quarter panel and my bars skidded down the passenger side leaving a bark buster-sized groove in his Landcruiser. Thank god for a good protective jacket because after a helicopter ride back into Cairns I was pretty much uninjured. I had a neck brace on for a week and a rock sock on my ankle. Renae wasn't impressed when I told her that I was going to play golf the following weekend because my club was hosting a comp that I didn't want to miss. Against doctor's orders, I took the neck brace and rock sock off for the game but I was still pretty stiff and was very careful to keep my head down, and I couldn't put any weight onto my ankle so it had actually created a better swing. I won the comp and came away with the prizes - "Beware the injured golfer".

Cornering

My number one rule for cornering is "Slow in – accelerate out!". I think this is the number one problem we encounter on tour, riders coming into corners way too hot. I think what happens is comparable to the dip story and the riders become complacent after experiencing a series of consistently similar corners on the trail. They fall into a false sense of security that the next one is going to be the same as the last ten they've just been through. Don't expect the next one to be the same as the last it could be a tricky switchback (180 degree curve) or there could be a vehicle coming in the other direction. If you can't see the exit of the corner than don't take it for granted that it's going to be the same as it was before.

CHAPTER 6

Horses for courses

Quite often the tourism businesses and cattle stations up in Cape York hire travellers to work with them through the busy tourist season. There's a long list of willing participants of the adventure-seeking kind that come from all over the world to spend some time in our remote outback communities. When it all dies down, they head back home before the wet season hits and you can't travel anywhere. It was pretty late in the season and all the traffic had died off almost completely. I was out with a mate exploring new tracks for a bit of an adventure when we came across a damsel sitting on the side of the road while her bike was also having a nap in the middle of the road. I asked her if everything was ok and she said, "Yes, everything is fine, I just can't pick it up". The bike was a BMW GS650 and she was in her sixties and just didn't have the strength to pick that bike up. I wonder how long she would have been sitting there if we hadn't just come along to offer assistance.

I get asked all the time which bike is best! There are so many variables to take into consideration. I can't name the best bike for you unless I ask a few questions first! Are you going to be riding on the tar, good gravel roads, are you aiming to hit some serious off-road sections, or are you planning a combination of them all? Is it going to be 30 degrees or -3? Are you going to be staying in the pubs and accommodation houses or are you going to be camping? Are you six-foot tall and 120 kilograms or are you five-foot and 60 kilos? Your size and skills need to be considered. You get the picture, right? I can tell you what helps me to make a decision and hope that it will help you to make your decision wisely.

So for me there are two main variables that go into a selection. When you're new to motorcycle adventure you might be nervous that you haven't got the skills to do some of the trails that you see in your local area, but let's not forget that the more you ride the better you will become. Once that sense of adventure hits the blood stream, your interest will grow and you will seek new trails to challenge your growing skill set. So let's not buy a motorcycle that is going to put a perimeter around your possibilities.

An adventure bike can be anything from a Postie Honda CT 110 up to a BMW GX1200 – that's all dependent on where you're going to go. Most people have their own preferences of bikes and sizes. Whether it be the capacity size of the bike or the brand of the bike that they desire most, there are so many die-hard brand loyalists and they're as one-eyed as a crazy football fanatic. They just can't see themselves riding anything else. Go for it I say. Buy what makes you happy. But some bikes are better for some jobs than others – for example, you wouldn't take a GS1200 to tackle the telegraph track but you would definitely take it on a trip similar to the Cairns to Darwin along the Savannah highway or any trip that has good off-road conditions. At the same time, taking a Postie Bike up the telegraph track is not such a good idea either. I've literally seen both of these situations and felt sorry for these fellas every time I saw them along the route, they're struggling in the sand and carrying the machines through the water and just generally not having any fun. I know it all sounds like a great idea when the boys are sitting in the shed having a few beers, but it's not until they're knee-deep in the mud and shit up the tele track that they realise what they've signed up for.

The technicality of your destination should determine the most suitable range of bikes for the purpose and what bikes are capable of doing the range of trails and tracks that you've decided to tackle. The things that are going to put limits on you are your budget, your skill level and the destination you seek. Do you need to ride it to work and use it for transportation or do you need to hide it from your wife in a mates shed?

Secondly the bike only needs to be adequate for you, don't be sucked into buying something that all your mates have just purchased like our damsel above. There's nothing sexy about riding around looking for somewhere to get your foot down or waiting around for someone to help you pick the bike up after you've dropped it. How quickly will your new friends change their minds about inviting you on the next ride if they are constantly babysitting? It's not about how fast you're going to get there or how many heads are going to turn as you ride past on the new weapon, "It's about getting to the destination – every time!". Be smart, take your time making the decision. It really is all about you here, your comfort and safety are paramount.

If you've decided that you're going for a pure dirt bike then power is the word. You're going to need power that's suited to your skill level. Don't be sucked in to an overpowered ride that is going to spit you off the back every time you roll on the throttle. Dirt bikes for fun are a big investment so go to any ride days that your local dealer is offering and test ride the bike beforehand if you can, or borrow a mate's bike and see how it rides. If you can't do any of these things then test it well in the bike shop. Sit and stand in all the positions that you think you're going to be in and see if the bike is comfortable. Make sure your feet can reach the ground in all the positions you think you're going to ride in. You don't have to be able to stand flat-footed over the bike but you do have to be able to get those tippy toes to reach. My bike is too tall for me theoretically but I have learned to swing a cheek off to get my toes down, so if you're confident to hang off your bike you can get the taller machine. If you're not confident than get a lower bike. When you're in a situation when stability is critical, like stopping or just being able to tap the ground to help straighten the bike, my top recommendation is the ability to touch the ground.

What I choose to ride now is the KTM 500 EXC because it is the sharpest tool in the shed. I customise my bike with a long range tank, Pivot Pegz, steering dampeners, bash plate and I make a few adjustments so the bike is adapted to me personally. I change the gearing to allow the bike to run on open sections a lot more easily and still have the capability to negotiate and explore all the tight trails that we do. Having spent so much time on a motorcycle, I'm a competent rider and this machine is capable, reliable and a fun bike for me to ride, the power makes me look good, I can just pop the front up anywhere that I want to. This bike suits my style of riding as I stand up a lot – the seat's like an ironing board so if you're going to sit on the bike it won't be so good for you. When I am choosing for our tour groups, with a wide range of shapes and skill levels, then I prefer to order a fleet of Suzuki DRZ400's because they are best suited to our terrain and they are very reliable- anyone can ride them and have a tonne of fun, from novice to expert alike.

The KTM 500 EXC is my preference for Cape York. It's a dirt bike but when we kick off the Cairns to Darwin rides next year I will be throwing my leg over the 790 adventurer, because it's more suited to an open highway of 3000 kms and the off-road gravel sections that are in that area. It's more comfortable over a longer period doing a lot more kilometres over the day but it will still handle the intermittent technical sections. I consider it as more of a dual-sport machine. This is the type of bike that will carry you to and from work, and if you ever wonder what's down that track en route, you will be able to go exploring on your way home of a Friday afternoon. The dual-sport range has seen a massive growth since my first bike; when I started touring Australia on my big adventure we were very limited in choices but Yamaha had just bought out the XT600 Tenerè. This was the first real adventure bike that was introduced into Australia. It was pretty exciting to see the set up that finally included a long range tank, a proven, reliable and powerful motor to enable mile munching on open stretches, a headlight that actually worked and wasn't just there for looks and a reasonably comfortable seat. It was the ideal horse for the course that I had imagined.

The big adventure bikes have one disadvantage, that being that they are generally quite tall, so ask your dealer if the bike you like has a lowering kit. This was a big factor when I chose the Suzuki DRZ650 for when we go to Darwin. They can be lowered, they're reliable, affordable and they're more comfortable for the longer miles we'll be doing.

When thinking about buying a bike you really have to make sure that you've got the budget to purchase, customise, register and insure it and then you have your ongoing maintenance that can sometimes trip you up in the budgeting. On a big adventure ride some bikes are more difficult to maintain and have serviced, so when making any decision take that into account. Look for simplicity in the routine maintenance like accessing the air filter box. Some bikes don't need any tools for this but others require tools and time to open them. Don't forget that you're going to need new tyres every so often and you'll need to change the oil as specified in the manual, then there is the occasional stack that's going to need attention to repair. Can you do these maintenance items by yourself or are you going to need help and how much is that going to cost? And just like any other vehicle we love, it will need to be insured, so think about what type of insurance will you take out for an adventure bike. All these things will make a huge difference to your decision-making process.

CHAPTER 7

Customising

In the cockpit

The adventure bikes these days are fairly well-kitted out for the purpose, with long-range fuel capacities and the creature comforts like heated grips, anti-lock braking systems, adjustable traction controls and even electronic suspension settings. All of these and more can be customised to handle the area you're riding in and to better suit your riding style and shape. For instance, if you're a tall guy and need some more room in the cockpit, you would bring the bars up as high and as far forward as you could, as opposed to a shorter guy who would do the opposite, adjusting the levers to where your fingertips lay naturally and comfortably.

One of the simplest, cheapest and most beneficial things you can change to improve your rider comfort are the handlebar grips. These come in all sorts of patterns and compounds, hard or soft. For example; you might have a bike that has a full waffle pattern all the way around the grip and if you're going to spend a lot of time in the saddle this pattern will create callouses and blisters on the palm of your hand. So you could opt for a gentler pattern with a soft feel grip that will absorb more vibration and protect your hands.

Handguards and bash plates

I don't like the flappy standard issue hand guards, they only really act as a wind guard and don't offer much protection at all. I much prefer to replace them with the Aussie made bark busters that have an aluminium bar through the middle of a hardened plastic cover. They just make me feel safer and ensure that if you do have a fall, you won't break your levers.

The bash plate provides insurance for your motor's engine cases from the elements. A lot of standard bikes come out with some sort of protection and most are generally plastic. Over the years I have hit some obstacles that have ripped these plastics off. I have found as good as they are, they tend to imprint into a rock or something that you might hit and rip off. I suggest using a good aftermarket aluminium bash plate, aluminium is more likely to slide over the offending object. There are a lot of different types that you can obtain for different models.

Seat height

So you've bought the bike and you're not happy with the stability because your feet don't reach the ground. There are a couple of things we can do here – firstly, you can get factory or aftermarket lowering kits for some models. These offer a change to the rear linkage arm that lowers the rear of the bike. Once that's in place you then loosen the triple clamp and slide the forks up through the triple clamp to re-balance the front height to match the rear of the bike. I personally don't like this set-up because it alters the geometry and handling of the bike away from its ultimate potential. Alternatively, you can alter the seat. Some manufacturers offer different height seats as an add-on purchase that have a lower design. Or you can get an upholsterer to remodify the standard seat for you. This feels more right to me to achieve the comfort zone and get your feet firmly on the ground.

Gearing

You can make changes to your external gearing, and what I mean by that is changing the size of the sprockets. This allows the motor to play its important role – it's the gearing that allows you to control the power of the motor in different conditions. This one customisation will improve the bikes performance and your ride experience.

The gearing is the amount of revolutions that the front sprocket turns the rear sprocket and therefore the wheel. To work out how many revolutions are in your set up, simply count the teeth on the driving (front) sprocket and divide it by the number of teeth on the driven (rear) sprocket.

Generally most of the standard motorcycles will come out with taller gearing. If you're going to do a lot of kilometres on the wide open roads you will want this taller gearing, making for a broader, slower response from the motor. With taller gearing your motor isn't working so hard at the higher speeds, and it will consume less fuel. But in a lot of off-road conditions and technical sections you're going to want to lower the gearing for the slower speeds that are required to negotiate cornering, creek crossing and sandy or rocky conditions. In slower conditions and ride speeds, the gearing needs to be lower to allow the motor to respond much faster to the rider's demands for power bursts.

It's best to experiment before going out on your adventure to find your happy medium. Try changing the front sprocket one or two teeth smaller and have a feel for what the bike does. Ask yourself if first gear is low enough to negotiate the more technical sections and then check if that top gear is happy to run at high speed on the open road without having the motor red lining. If you're not sure, ask your bike dealer for assistance because he will know what is best suited for the model that you have.

Fuel Range

On one occasion a friend, who was a motorcycle magazine journalist, and I were out to write an article. It was just him and I on this particular ride and we were on our way home on a long transport section. Because we are mates we were always having a go at each other and spurring the other one on. We are both experienced riders and our games reflect that and I would not recommend you play these pranks on a new rider. So we were riding and riding when he decided he needed a distraction

CUSTOMISING

and I was targeted. He came up behind me and hit the kill switch on my bike – that's pretty funny when it happens once. He wasn't familiar with the location and had full faith in me to get us from point 'A' to point 'B' without putting much thought into how we were getting there – perfect! That was to my advantage so I decided to bide my time and not retaliate. He thought this was quite odd behaviour from me but kept pushing my buttons. He'd scream up next to me when he thought I wasn't watching and kill my engine and speed away to get out in front as I lost momentum, restarted the bike and got going again. After a few repetitions of this I decided to let him stay out front, which is totally against my nature, and I just kept the pressure on to make him worry. I waited for my moment to take the lead again and get out front but this time I wasn't letting him anywhere near my kill switch because my prank was about to begin. I pointed to him to get his full attention, then I pointed to my long-range fuel tank and then back at his standard fuel tank, smiling and waving him goodbye. Sure enough, within a kilometre he had a push bike and I was sitting in the pub having a beer.

Not all bikes will come out with long range tanks that give enough fuel range for your destination. There are a few different manufacturers that make a varied range of tanks to suit different models. For instance, our DRZ's don't have a long-range tank so we have chosen to run the 17-litre safari tanks that are most appropriate for what we do. You can buy 25-litre tanks but I find that these weigh us down and add too much bulk to the front of the bike. The 17-litre suits us best and gets us from one fuel stop to the next without having to carry any excess. We have been using Safari tanks for a number of years and they have proven to be reliable. They're tough – real tough. They have been crashed tested by quite a few dummies and have never let us down.

In any case I would recommend popping on an in-line fuel filter or two if your tank has two taps. Make sure you have a good in-line fuel filter on your bike because I've had problems over the years with dirty fuel where the sources are less reliable in remote areas. It's particularly more important when most of the bikes these days that are fuel injected require really clean fuel. You can get these from any automotive store.

Pivot Pegz

Pivot Pegz are my next go-to piece of bling for my bike. They are a state-of-the-art foot peg with wide 60-millimetre resting platform that keeps you in constant contact with the bike. They have a super grip pattern that offers traction under foot, and a spring-loaded pivoting action. If you're changing position on the bike from standing to sitting then your ankle and foot are always changing angles. The Pivot Pegz twist around a heavy duty self-adjusting spring that regulates the motion of this change in position. This all equates to a superior grip and load distribution and no more slips off the peg. Not only do they take out the vibration between the foot peg and your boot that is very fatiguing on the legs, they also help maintain longevity in the soul of your boot. These are an Aussie design and manufactured product – ask your motorcycle dealer.

Clean air

I think the most important part of maintaining any motor is keeping the air flow clean. This simple practice will create longevity in your motor. Fine dust particles can find their way through the motor and destroy any moving parts in its path. The particles work their way through the carburettor, valves, into the cylinder and eventually foul up the engine oil. This leads to wear and tear in the gear box and big end – the biggest killer of any engine! Checking and cleaning your air filter after each ride will give your bike a longer life and greater fuel efficiency. It will require less oil changes and maintenance. People are reluctant to do this chore because it is tedious and messy, but let me remind you that it does save money and mechanical problems on the trail.

Remove the filter, clean it and set it out to dry. Use a good foam filter oil and once the foam filter is placed back on to its frame, we usually smear some grease around the edge of the filter where it seats back into the air filter box, as this gives a good seal and prevents any air leaking through any deformities in the filter.

Additionally we place an air filter skin over our filters. This is a stocking type fabric that covers the whole filter and acts as a pre-filter before the standard foam filter. Depending on where I'm off to, I sometimes opt to use a couple of pre-filters or skins. Just make sure you're not starving the motor of oxygen though. Filter skins are convenient on long, multi-day rides because you can just peel one off as required as opposed to carrying everything you need to clean a foam one. It's a simple hack that makes easier work of the maintenance while out on the trail. These skins can be sourced from your motorcycle shop. Keep your filter clean and your bike will give you fewer hassles, last longer and save you money.

Tyre pressure

Tyre pressure is one of the key things that you can adjust along the way that will help you get the most out of your ride. I am constantly changing the pressure in my tyres to suit the terrain that I am in. Rock hard tyre pressure makes you lose traction on slippery or loose terrain like sand, gravel or mud. You have to let your tyres down to get the grip you need. Letting the tyres down will flatten the curve of the tyre and create a bigger footprint, giving you extra stability. Lower your tyre pressure when the terrain is loose and slippery and you'll gain more control. You need a higher pressure in your tyres in rocky conditions or any conditions that have hard obstacles like tree routes, boulders or bulldust holes with sharp edges. Higher pressure is for higher speeds and hard surfaces so as to avoid the tyre from being pinched against the rim. This will vary depending on what type of bike and how much it weighs and how much gear you are carrying so adjust the pressure to suit.

The exhaust

I change the standard muffler on my bike to an aftermarket titanium one mainly to save some weight and to assist with some extra performance. It's not as restrictive as the standard muffler and the motor can breathe better. Of course it sounds better with a deeper and nicer note but NOT to make it louder. I've seen too many people with aftermarket mufflers that are far too loud. It's so annoying and can you imagine sitting on the bike and listening to that for 1000 kilometres? Not only will you piss off the local community but you risk making yourself deaf. These mufflers are not cheap and for most people I've seen, it's just a bit of bling, if you're not seeking extra performance than stick with the standard muffler.

Saddle bags and panniers

If you are going to be using saddle bags or panniers you'll have to make a decision about whether to choose the hardened suitcase type or the soft duffle bag type. It's a personal preference really and there are pros and cons for each. In any case make sure they are waterproof. That might be more of a pro for the soft choices because any drop on a hard case is going to break the seal and you'll need waterproof liners to keep them viable.

CUSTOMISING

When packing make sure any heavy items like a bottle of bourbon should be at the bottom to disperse the top weight of the bike. Just think of your packing so that the heaviest items go in the lowest positions and the lightest items go up high so that you're not top-heavy and making the bike harder to handle.

Simplify your packing so that the items you need at night are in one case, then you can unclip one and go into your hotel room instead of hauling the lot. It's also handy when you're at a campsite to just take one bag to the showers with you. This is, of course, unless you're in a dodgy part of town and it's likely to get knocked off.

If you can, try to leave some room on your bike or in your backpack to bring special finds home. We've got this awesome beach run that we do in certain times of the year. It's 70 kilometres of wild beach that's open to the Coral Sea. Beachcombing is sure to find you a treasure here and we've seen the most incredible things washed up. I found a message in a bottle once. The note was written in pencil to prevent any ink from leaking on the page, it was wrapped around a cigar to absorb any water and sealed tight with a real cork. It had come from Club Med in France and was dated six years prior to when I found it. I tried to make contact with the writer but he had moved on from that location. The second message was sent in a Jim Beam bottle with no care and read, "If you find this please refill and send back with big-breasted blonde".

We've found true glass buoys that have washed off fishing trawlers from all over the world. I've found lengths of heavy shipping braid and brought it back to decorate the shed into a beach house. That was interesting to be sure, I sat on my bike and had the other boys wrap the rope around me. Now I'm not talking any old rope – this one had at least a ten centimetre diameter and had been rolling around in the sand for years. It was heavy, really heavy and I felt like the Michelin man on a dirt bike. My support driver wasn't too happy about working around this treasure for the next few days, he had to take it out every time to get into the truck and it dropped kilos of sand every time he did – sorry mate!

I've found an army box that had washed off an American vessel during a war game practice exercise. DO NOT OPEN THESE if you find them. I did - kicked the lock off it with my boot – and the missiles rolled into the lid as it fell open. I took photos and reported it to the authorities. My photos couldn't differentiate between a white or grey band and it very nearly got me a ride in a Blackhawk helicopter as the navy wanted me to escort them to the exact spot where I had left the box. However, the tragic incident in Townsville occurred in the week before our planned mission to fly up to Cape York and the boys ended up driving. I didn't have that much spare time so I drew them a map. They found the box and called me to report that they were in fact dummies. Phew!

On another occasion we found an odd little canister that had something rattly inside. The lid was fused shut so I chucked it in my backpack and brought it home. I popped it on a shelf and forgot all about it until I saw it on television a few months later. I called the number on the tele and within half an hour the place was surrounded by police cars, fire engines and big fellas in hazmat suits. It turns out that the canister contained the highly toxic chemical aluminium phosphide, and they'd been turning up on Queensland beaches for quite some time. I wasn't prepared for that on a Friday afternoon.

This beach was peppered with beautiful seashells and I loved the nautilus. I would search high and low for a whole one. You see, Renae's birthday is in September and I have been on tour for all but one over the last 30 years, so the least I could do was bring her home a beautiful shell. She absolutely loved it and it made her cry to think that I had thought of her while I was out on tour. So I bought her one every year and she put them up on the mantel in our bathroom. Every year I came home from the September trip and happily said, "I bought you a present". I think it was number three when she said, "If it's another @#$% shell, you can keep it". She's so ungrateful! It takes a lot of care to bring them home in one piece.

CUSTOMISING

Anyway the moral of the story is, save some room for important things and wives like to change it up a bit for their birthdays apparently.

CHAPTER 8

Shit happens

I am going to cover off on a few mechanical problems that you could encounter on any multi-day adventure ride. These 'Bush Mechanics' are for the mechanically-minded reader that works on his/her own bike at home and wants to be self-sufficient out on the trail. We use DRZ 400's so the tips are written to suit these bikes but you can adjust the idea to suit your machine of choice. Being self-sufficient sometimes means being creative – learn your machine and the creativity will follow. **These tips are aimed to be a temporary fix to get you home, and they are not meant to stay in place in the long term.**

So it's hard to predict what's going to happen and foresee into the future of your adventure ride but there are some pretty common things that you might think of; flat tyres, broken chain, putting a stick through your radiator, but there are also irregular things that could happen.

My throttle cable broke one day and the bike rolled to a slow stop. Luckily I wasn't too far from home but it was too bloody far to walk and I still had to get myself back. The cable was broken about a foot down from where it mounts to the throttle and the only thing I could think of at the time was to take the outer skin 'of' the cable – 'off' the cable – to expose the inner cable to give me just enough length to thread up between the tank and my seat. I was thinking that at least I had access to it with my hand.

In my head, the theory all sounded great and it worked like a charm. I could manually pull up on the cable to open the throttle with my right hand and still be able to operate the clutch with my left and I'd be able to get moving again. However, it wasn't very elegant as I realised that you have to be an absolute surgeon to get the timing right. It was a hair trigger with the slightest touch shooting me straight into full throttle. It was not at all what I had expected, the bike was screaming off while I was trying to wrangle it with the other less dominant hand. It made for an interesting afternoon in any case.

So after doing surgery for a while and hacking away at my patience, trying to smooth the power out with a chunk of cable in my hand, I decided it was all too erratic and it was time to change tactics. I ended up getting a tyre lever out of my bumbag because I needed to get some leverage on this cable and slow the action down, or at least make it less sensitive. I tied the cable one third of the way up the tyre lever and jimmied the tyre lever between the seat and the tank so I could grip the longer end in my hand. Thankfully that gave me a little more control and eventually got me home.

Nowadays nearly all bikes have dual-throttle cables running to the handle for safety reasons – one for opening and one for returning should the throttle get stuck open. If this was to happen to you, you could use the other cable to switch over to the pull by re-routing the cable to suit. Bush mechanics-style, you have to use your head to figure that out depending on which bike you have. Something as simple as a throttle cable can end your adventure just like this. You can't really pack all the spares you think you might need, that would just weigh you down. If you have a fairly new bike it shouldn't be an issue but if you have a bike that is two or more years old I would be looking into carrying spare throttle and clutch cables just to be on the safe side, or check and replace them before you go.

Wheel bearings

Wheel bearings are another overlooked item. Make sure you check them by trying to move the wheel from side to side and pack them with grease. Even though you've done this, it doesn't mean they will last the duration of your ride. These items don't take up much room so take a spare set with you. It might make all the difference to your ride.

Wheel balancing

Balancing your wheels has a big effect on any motorcycle. Not only does it make the ride a lot smoother but it also prolongs the life of the moving parts; tyre, chain, sprockets, wheel bearings and linkage system for the rear swing arm – and on top of that it will decrease rider fatigue. If you don't have a wheel balanced on an extended ride, the weight of the rim lock and the valve on the wheel will create a high spot that causes a hammering movement. The hammering movement wears the tyre into an egg shape. You can imagine what this feels like, riding down the road on an oblong wheel. It's only slight but the vibrations will be enhanced.

I worked this out a long time ago. Sometimes I have to meet up with a group at the opposite end of the Cape to where I am and I have to get there on a deadline. I'll take the most direct route, which includes a section of the old telegraph track, and has me sitting on high speed sections for hours on end. On one ride my back wheel started vibrating to the point where the number plate cracked so I pulled in to see a friend at a roadhouse halfway down the journey. He had a workshop with a tyre machine and balance weights for cars only. I used them to balance the wheel, the car weights were wrong for the motorbike but we made them work by wiring them on to the spokes. Even though the tyre was already worn to this egg shape the balancing weights smoothed out the rest of my ride dramatically.

You can do this at home. You just need a vice, then place the axel into the vice horizontally and slide the wheel on. Spin the tyre and where it settles to a stop you will then add a counter weight to the opposite side (the top side of where it settles). This doesn't have to be one weight but could be three or four, depending on how many are required. You can get weights from your dealer and they either adhere to the rim or attach to the spokes. Try to get the balance as close as possible.

You can also balance the tyre while it is attached to the motorcycle as long as there is no friction from the disc pads or the disc, just disconnect the rear chain from the sprocket. The wheel needs to be on the axel with no other causes of friction and you can repeat the process as above. Alternatively, get your dealer to do it when you get the tyres changed.

The chain

You can't adjust the chain while it's on the stand and static – you have to be sitting on it to get the proper tension. To get the correct adjustment you will have to be sure to check the chain while the bike is fully loaded, including you. Pack the bike with everything you're going to be carrying and then sit on the bike, lean over from the seated position and wiggle the chain up and down to make sure that you have about 20 millimetres of free play.

I get asked repeatedly if you should "oil your chain regularly or leave it to dry out". The thought is that oiling regularly will encourage the build-up of debris like sand and dust on the chain which is then going to produce wear and tear on the sprockets and pins. There is no doubt in my mind that this is not true. Oiling your chain regularly actually prolongs the life of the chain and gearing. What you're actually doing is lubricating the seals. Whether it be an O-ring or an X-ring chain, oiling seals the inner pin from getting dirt and dust in it. So it's not the fact that there is oil externally on the chain to lessen the friction between the chain roller and the sprocket – its primary role is to protect and seal those inner pins of the chain rollers.

Some of the latest and bigger adventure bikes don't have this issue because they are shaft driven so nothing is exposed to the elements. Shaft drives are clean and fairly robust but they also require some maintenance and regular oil changes and to check for any water that may have penetrated and mixed with the oil. The cons that I have experienced are that they are expensive and heavy and if they fail along the way there is no quick fix to get you going again.

The flat – tube tyres

One of the most common and obvious problems is a flat tyre. Most of you have had experience in this area and everybody has their own ideas on how to change it the quickest. There are a few little tricks to make it all run smoothly and hopefully prevent any more occurrences. Having the right equipment will go a long way: If you fail to prepare, prepare to fail.

When travelling, you are limited for space, so what you carry is the key. It is common to take a front and rear tube with a puncture repair kit. However, I have found that the front is more likely to go first. I pack two front tubes. You can run the front tube in a rear tyre if necessary but it doesn't work in reverse.

Prevention

Running the correct tyre pressure, using heavy duty tubes and reading the terrain – being careful of the objects that you're likely to hit – will help prevent a majority of flat tyres. Even with every precaution being taken it's inevitable that you will get a flat tyre one day.

When you're on an adventure bike you don't want to lay it on its side to change the flat because it's fully laden with the equipment that you've brought along, so while it's on the side stand loosen the axel nut, the rim lock that holds the bead onto the rim and loosen the valve stem nut. Yes, do these things first and I will tell you why shortly. Just loosen them for now.

Look for a sturdy branch that you can break into around a two-foot length – that sharp-toothed saw comes in handy doesn't it? Use the stick to prop the bike up from the opposite side of the stand. Pick the bike up a bit and wedge the stick into the under carriage of the bike. We're trying to make a tripod of the side stand, the stick and the good tyre. It only has to be tall enough to get the flat tyre off the ground. Once you've cleared the wheel from the ground and you're satisfied that the bike is sturdy, well sturdy enough, you can pull the loosened axel out. Now if you hadn't loosened the axel nut prior you'd be applying pressure to the makeshift stand and I can tell you from experience that it is going to fall every time.

Don't lose your small parts. There's nothing worse than getting through the full tyre change, sweating like you've been swimming, watching the sun go down and trying to find lost nuts in the fading light. I always put my axel in the muffler so it doesn't get any debris on it and it doesn't grease up my bumbag or whatever I would have placed it on. It's just a cleaner option and it offers the axel the protection it needs.

Lay your wheel on the ground, disk side UP, or you run the risk of bending it when you're jumping all over the rim through the repair process. Break the bead all the way around before you apply the tyre levers. When you've got a flat the bead has usually worked its way off the rim but in some cases it can be easier said than done. If you're having trouble, use the heel of your boot and all your weight, and if that still doesn't work and you happen to be riding with a buddy you can use his side stand and lever the weight of his bike to break the bead.

I see so many guys having trouble when it comes time to put the levers in because they usually put one lever in and prise the tyre up off the rim. This creates a hell of a lot more tension around the bead and it makes it very hard to get the second lever in. The tiny vice is not going to accept the second lever without a serious amount of force and energy. Put both levers in at the same time while the bead is loose, space them about 3-4 inches apart and now when you pull back on the first lever your second lever is already in place. This makes the hardest part of the tyre change a lot smoother and easier. I lock my lever in under the disc and it stays in place while I move the second lever around the bead in three-inch sections, peeling the tyre off the rim gradually.

If you do have a flat, it is essential to find the cause. One common and usually overlooked problem that causes recurring flats is the failure to check the inner casing of the tyre. Always make sure that it hasn't been torn internally by a sharp object or that it doesn't still have that sharp object in there. A tear in the tyre casing will chew away at a new tube in less than 100 kilometres and you'll have to change it again. If you have got a tear in the tyre casing you can minimise the effects by using the old damaged tube that's coming out. Cut along the centre rib of the tube, remove the valve stem and you've created a sleeve for the new tube to sit in. This will get you home. I like to conserve energy wherever I can so before I put the new tube into the sleeve and the tyre I always remove the valve and blow the tyre up with my lungs until it creates its shape but is still pliable. This tip will prevent excess pumping and pinching of the tube when levering the tyre back onto the rim. Then I replace the valve before inserting the new tube into the tyre – pump it up to your desired pressure. I would run a higher pressure to minimise any movement of that split of the tyre casing. Invest in a CO_2 adapter and always have bottles on hand, because who wants to be pumping air into a tyre by hand these days? Having said that, I always carry a compact bicycle pump for back up.

Now that the tube is in the tyre and you've pushed and worked in as much of the bead as you can with your boots, kneel down on either side of the tyre. Where the bead is seated you can start slowly levering the tyre back on. This is a crucial time to be very aware not to pinch the tube as you're working. We all have and will continue to do it but take a moment to get it right, take your time. I can't tell you how many times I've done a whole change only to discover that I've pinched the tube on levering and had to start again – it's deflating!! Haha.

When levering the tyre on be sure not to take the lever past a 90-100 degree angle. Push down with your free hand to get the bead to reseat into the rim. Going past the 90-degrees is what causes the lever to pick up the tube and pinch it against the rim. This is slower but it ensures that you won't have to do it twice.

When you get to the last little section, which is the most difficult being the tightest part of the bead to get on, try not to pull your lever out. Lower it down toward the disc but keep it tucked in to the tyre, use the heel of your free hand to punch the lever around a few extra millimetres tucking the bead and levering upward to the 90-degree again as you go. Repeat until it's in place.

The flat - tubeless tyres

Tubeless tyres are more common on the modern adventure bikes these days and they have their pros and cons. The unsprung weight is beneficial to the suspension and being able to use a plug kit for minor holes is a big advantage. However, if you cut the tyre on a sharp rock or tree root you won't have any options unless you're carrying a spare tyre.

I've heard plenty of stories and people swearing by the bush mechanic tip that you can pack a tubeless tyre full of grass and it will get you home. Nope, this does not work, I have tried it! You'd need a bloody workshop press to make that work. So my get out of jail free card here is to carry heavy duty zip ties that you can place around the rim and the tyre, evenly spaced out to a minimum of about six inches (add more if you have them) and zip them up all the way around the circumference. If you ride accordingly this will help you to get you to the next place of safety.

Fuel injection

The way of the future. A lot of people ask me, "Is it better than carburetted bikes?". Absolutely, there is no doubt in my mind. This is for a number of reasons. I don't want to bore you with my whole perspective but it has been around for a very long time, is fuel-efficient and has been proven to be very reliable and definitely improves the performance of the motor. The perception is that the carburetted bike is better because it is mechanically operated and can be pulled apart to be fixed or cleaned versus the fuel-injection system that is more electrically operated that most people are afraid they can't fix.

When you're riding in remote areas, some of these service stations are going to have low consumption rates and infrequent top ups, so that fuel is going to be stored for quite some time. It's not always stored in the best of housing and it's going to build up particles and debris that will be going straight into your tank. If your bike starts running badly with a lack of power and inconsistent throttle response it could mean that the fuel injector is semi-blocked or blocking up. It's important to check the flow of fuel between the tank and the fuel pump. If the fuel is not flowing at all, clean the in-tank filters.

I have found that pressurising the fuel line with compressed air, while hitting the start button at the same time, opens the injector.

This will usually clear a lot of the debris and allow the bike to run properly again. I've made one out of a tyre valve adapter that allowed me to insert the nozzle into the fuel line and blast it with compressed air. If you have a fuel injected bike maybe think about getting an adapter for a CO_2 bottle to do this job. Running an extra in line fuel filter is highly recommended on fuel-injected bikes for an adventure ride in remote areas.

Secondly, check that the fuel pump is working. Most bikes will have a diaphragm-type fuel pump that primes itself every time you turn the bike on, so listen closely and see if you can hear the pump in action. If you can't hear it, then you've pretty much isolated the problem. It's likely to be one of two things in this instance. One, the pump has deteriorated internally or excess wear and tear have destroyed it, or two, you have a broken circuit or electrical fault that means power is not getting to the fuel pump. If there is no power getting to the pump, check for loose or corroded connections, loose or broken wires, blown fuses etc. If you're lucky a contact-cleaner and some buffing of the contacts might be enough to get the pump working again, but if this doesn't work you may need to change the contacts or buy a whole new pump.

River crossings

Living in Tropical North Queensland with an annual rainfall of seven metres (not seven inches, seven METRES!) we're fairly used to experiencing high amounts of water out on the trail. Like I've said before, the depth can be deceiving, especially when they are crystal clear; you definitely need to walk them first to clarify and establish which line you are going to take. Another reason for walking the crossing is to check the bottom you will be riding on. Is it slippery, are there big boulders submerged, is there any current and how strong is it?

Double-checking the current will give vital information. Walking across on your own and walking a bike across the current is very different, your legs will not cause much resistance but the bike acts like a sheet and causes plenty. Once committed to the crossing, this resistance makes the bike become really heavy. You run the risk of submerging the bike or losing it downstream.

This has happened to me on a few different occasions and I've seen it happen so many times to other riders, and it always gets the heart racing. We were out on a group ride about 150 kilometres shy of Kowanyama heading toward Darwin when we came across a causeway that looked calm. There was water over the concrete that had a glassy surface and no signs of flow, right up until you were about a third of the way across it. That was when you'd feel the angle of your bike start to decline as the water force tried to push your wheels out from under you. The causeway was smooth and hard on the upstream side but the current had eaten away at the structure on the downstream side. The concrete was crumbling and the foundations were exposed. It took all my body weight and a good argument with the bike to get it across. I had a few minutes before the next rider came along so I called the support vehicle to set up a lunch stop, sensing that we might be there for a while. A few riders came through and, given the hand signals and warning to go high, they came through, struggling but safe. The third rider came in hot, sticking to his side of the road and causing a bow wave that caught him off guard. He hit the grits and over the edge he went. The bike bobbed once and disappeared and we watched a helmet bob and gurgle under and then a boot appeared and our panic rose. As I ran downstream to catch sight of him, tow rope in hand, he managed to get a foot to floor and stand up. God love him, he still had a grip on the bike, what a legend! So we de-drowned the bike while the crew had a hearty lunch and all was well in the world again.

SHIT HAPPENS

So you've determined the depth and which line to take. Now, which style will you choose? Are you going to ride the bike, walk the bike with the motor running or push the bike with the motor off? My rule of thumb is: if the water is axle-deep you can ride across. If it is wheel-deep I'll walk the bike in first gear, remembering to be on the downstream side of the bike. If it is seat-deep then it's obvious to walk across with the engine off. This should keep you out of trouble.

Water proofing

Standard bikes are not set up for creek crossings and some models only have to look at water before they stall.

Carburetted bikes

You can make some waterproofing adjustments by re-routing the breather hoses from the carburettor and the engine. On most bikes the original engine breather route is down low, between the engine case and the swing arm. When you are crossing water, the engine will cool, which creates a vacuum that sucks the water up through the breather and into the carbie and the engine. These two minor adjustments change the whole manner of the bike and allow it a greater ability to handle depths of water. Re-direct the black engine hose up high, to the air filter box, and the two hoses (or four in some models) from the side of the carburettor somewhere high underneath the seat or fuel tank. Not all of the hoses from the carbie need to be re-routed; leave the drain hoses from the bottom as they are. Fuel-injected bikes obviously don't have this issue so there's another advantage.

De-drowning

We've all done it, it's as easy as losing your footing on a slippery rock and the bike gets totally submerged. Do not try to start it, as the engine is like a blender and will mix the water with the oil immediately. Open the air filter box and take the filter out. Squeeze the water out and leave it to dry. Turn the fuel off and open the drain on the carbie and leave it open. Water will have worked its way into the engine cases. If you haven't started the bike the water will not have mixed with the oil, as water is heavier than oil and will sink to the bottom. To remove this water, crack the oil drain plug and carefully unscrew it slowly until water starts to seep out. Do NOT remove the plug or you will lose all your oil as well. Once the water is dribbling out, let it go on until oil starts to seep through. Then you will know that most of the water has been removed and you can do the oil drain plug back up. Once you've removed the water from the engine cases the motor is safe to wind over. Remove the spark plug and with the throttle wide open wind the motor over until all the water stops pumping out of the cylinder head. Replace the spark plug. Now you're right to start the bike safely. Do up the carbie drain, turn the fuel back on, replace the dry air filter and do up the box. Again, I stress that there is no shortcut to this system. If you push or tow the bike to start you will run the risk of causing severe damage. Take the time to do it right and it will ensure that you can keep riding.

So this is all well and good for a single cylinder bike but some of the new multi-cylinder bikes are a little more complex. The same theory applies but the accessibility to spark plugs is a lot more interesting. I found myself in this very predicament one day when I was out doing a trip around the Gulf country with a television personality. We had very certain deadlines because of the show and they had been sponsored to test ride a certain motorcycle. During the set-up phase of the ride I specifically asked the manager if he had some tools for me to be able to access the spark plug should we have any water issues along the way. He insisted that "these bikes are like submarines and you won't need that Roy".

You guessed it, we did need it! This particular crossing was too deep to ride and the bikes were certainly too heavy to carry and because we were on a deadline we had to get to the other side. Our only option was to push them with the engines off and pray.

A quick hit on the start button confirmed they were full of water. Water does not compress and the cylinder locked. If you ever find yourself in this predicament DO NOT try to tow or bump start the bikes because you will do serious damage to the motor.

I proceeded to strip the bike to get to the spark plugs thinking I might have something in my tool bag that could possibly fit. When I took the spark plug cap off the first cylinder, I could see the spark plug was a foot deep in the hole and there was no way I was going to get to it without that specific tool I'd requested. What to do???

We had no choice but to set up camp for the night while I worked out how to de-drown these bikes.

So my thought process evolved and I figured that you can't compress water, so if we used the start button EVER SO GENTLY we could pressurise the cylinder and trap the water, forcing it to slowly work its way past the piston and rings and into the engine case, thus emptying that cylinder of water. These bikes had three cylinders (some will have two) so we waited for half an hour or more before pressing the start button to activate the second cylinder and then waited again to activate the third cylinder.

We had four bikes to do this process on so the time went pretty quickly and we let it settle overnight so all the water could make its way into the engine case.

The next morning I undid the oil drain plug on the engine until the water started to empty out and kept it unscrewed until oil started coming through before doing it up again. We changed the air filters for the dry spares that we had and hit the button. Thankfully they all came to life straight away and we were right back on our filming schedule again.

SHIT HAPPENS

Radiators

While the advancing technology in motorcycles is leaping and bounding forward a lot of trail riders are being left behind in the field. What I mean by that is, as the bikes become more advanced, less riders know how to fix them. One such problem comes from water-cooled motorcycles with radiators. Having run water-cooled bikes through Cape York for the last couple of decades we have encountered our fair share of problems on the track. I know what you're thinking and YES there are aftermarket guards for radiators that help support and strengthen them, but while these products are a help they can also hinder the cooling. These products can make the cooling system 30% less efficient and that really matters when temperatures are high. Trail riding is all about being out in the middle of nowhere and if you encounter a damaged radiator you really need to know how to get the bike and yourself home. A damaged radiator can happen from any number of unfortunate events, like piercing caused by a tree branch or a rock, but more commonly damage is caused from a come-off that lays the bike on its side and crushes the radiator or a tear that will leak.

One important thing to remember is: if you have an impact-damaged radiator from a crash and it is not leaking, do not try to straighten it as the fatigue in the metal will crack – if it is not leaking do not fix it. The first and easiest fix is to carry some liquid steel; this is easily sourced from your local hardware store. Liquid steel is handy for all sorts of repairs to engine cases and a cracked radiator with a minimal leak.

If you have a radiator that is bent or broken beyond repair and it is leaking in multiple areas, you can run the bike home on one radiator if you plumb it correctly – different models are plumbed differently but with a bit of common sense, or rather imagination, you can analyse the routing and figure out how the system works.

On most bikes there are usually two hoses from the engine to the radiators, one from the water pump to the top of the right-hand radiator and the second being the one that connects between the bottom of the left-hand radiator to the cylinder head of the engine. There are also two interconnecting hoses that link the bottoms and tops of the radiators to each other. This varies from different manufacturers/models but is achievable in most cases.

To eliminate one radiator you need to re-plumb the water pump to the top of the working radiator where the interconnecting hose would normally go, and the bottom hose of the good radiator to the cylinder head of the engine. You might be left with loose ends that need to be plugged or crimped; these are the interconnection hoses between left and right radiators. I normally carry a rubber bung in my bumbag that makes this easy to do but a whittled down stick can work well if you need it to. Once you are satisfied that you have plumbed the good radiator correctly and tied off all loose ends you need to fill it. This process depends on which side you are using. You will either have a cap which you would fill as normal, or on the other side you will have a bleeder nut – loosen the nut, and use the top interconnection hose to fill the radiator with water until it flows from the bleeder nut. Crimp the interconnecting hose and tighten the bleeder nut. You can use creek water to fill it if you are lucky enough to have one handy like we normally do, otherwise use the water in your camelback as a last resort.

If you have a small hole or crack you can use the old bush mechanic trick of putting pepper in your radiator – who carries pepper while trail riding right? You can get this specialised product in a small canister from the radiator repair shops, it takes up no room and doesn't add any weight so it's a good little extra to have. It is somehow magnetically drawn to the hole and swells to seal it.

CHAPTER 9

Dress for the occasion

Colours

The number one reason to wear riding gear is to protect your skin, muscles and bones in a crash, but the second is to increase your chances of being seen by other road users. The brighter or lighter the gear you choose the better chance you have of being seen, especially if the conditions are crap with poor light or bad weather.

Helmets

I read on a helmet box one day that inside was a brain protection system. I thought that was a pretty funny way to say it but OK, I agree a helmet is seriously important. Make sure to choose one that conforms to the Australian standards, and buy the highest safety ratings in your budget range. Then it's all about fit – a helmet should have a firm snug fit on your cheeks and full contact around your noggin. There shouldn't be any pressure points anywhere, especially on the peak of your hairline at your forehead. Any pressure points will only increase in size and irritation throughout a trip with the friction of movement and vibration caused by riding. Put the helmet on and do it up to check for comfort, then swivel your head from side to side and make sure that your vision range is never compromised. I like the helmets that have a face shield and pull-down visor for extended touring on adventure bikes. Be sure to protect your eyes and use a clear visor or goggles for night, choose a shatterproof material and protect it from scratches. You can't see well if you're looking through a buffed-up lens.

Neck braces

I think they are a great idea to protect both the neck and collarbones. The collarbone is the most common injury that I have seen over the years and it happens when the rider's head hits the ground and the base of the helmet is forced into the collar bone. I haven't yet moved into using a neck brace because I have a short neck and it doesn't work for me. I find that they hamper my movement and the limited swivel restricts my vision.

Music

When I was on the Tenerè heading around Australia I was very high tech and had a walkman cassette player in the pocket of my jacket so I could listen to music while I was riding. I recall listening to Meatloaf's Bat Out of Hell and as the beat got higher and more demanding so too did my pace on the bike. I was so enthralled in the music that that was where my attention laid and I ended up over-shooting a corner before I even saw it coming. These days we have all kinds of really good communication systems – bluetooth music from your phone for example, which also let you make phone calls along the way, intercoms to talk to other riders are common as well – and all these fantastic devices make riding long transport sections a lot more enjoyable. However, you have to be mindful to listen to the traffic and your bike. Concentrate on the road and the terrain areas that you're in. I'd go as far as to say not to use them when you're in technical sections that need your full concentration.

Earplugs

I like to wear earplugs if I'm going to be doing any long-haul section just to help protect my drums from extended periods of noise or any wind vibration that might make its way into my helmet.

Gloves

Your hands are often the first thing that's going to hit the ground if you ever crash or fall, so it's really important to have a comfortable and protective pair of gloves on at all times. Check that they have a reinforced palm, knuckle protection and Velcro closure around the wrists so they won't come off.

Jackets

Riding gear has come a long way from the old oil infused Belstaff jacket with newspaper packing to keep you warm. The modern jackets these days are designed for all sorts of different weather and climactic conditions, but in many cases though it's a fact that you will get what you pay for. They are expensive but so are ambulance rides and hospital vacations to fix what's been broken. The waterproof jackets with woollen liners won't be suited to tropical or hot locations so we opt for the ventilated, quick-dry denier nylon or Gore-Tex types that have breathable mesh panels for comfort. I personally think that any gear made from Gore-Tex is best because they are highly resistant to abrasion and tears, and will protect you from the elements while allowing your skin to breath and release perspiration. Anything plastic will do the opposite and lock in your body heat and sweat and will make you really uncomfortable.

I highly suggest a jacket with body armour and elbow pads to give you the best protection, or at a minimum with elbow and shoulder guards – unlike the cover shot that was purely taken for a reason! Be sure that it's comfortable because you're going to be in this gear for a long time, so don't sacrifice comfort for the overly extreme safety options that can be really heavy. You don't want to be irritated and blistered every day that you wear the gear. Make sure it is comfortable in the bike shop before you leave and wear it in to be doubly sure before departing on your grand adventure. A higher level of protection will make you feel more confident when you're riding and that's what we want to feel when we're out there.

Pants

Pants with built in knee guards are my preferred method of protecting your legs. You can have pants and knee guards or a knee-brace combinations for particular reasons. The main thing here is if you are going to encounter water you don't want a cloth or leather style that will hold the moisture and buff you up. Nylon or Gore-Tex are far better options but knee protection is an ultimate must here because the lower your body is to the road the closer you are to the elements that are going to cause injury. I've had my knee guards split by a rock that was flicked up by a passing vehicle and they saved my knee.

DRESS FOR THE OCCASION

Boots

Being the closest thing to the ground your foot and ankle need the most protection, and that can only be provided by your boots. I see people coming on tour with their ankle-high steel cap work boots. They get a bit upset with me when I tell them that they aren't appropriate and try to hand them a pair of knee-high off-road motorcycle boots. They tell me that they are more comfortable in their own boots for all sorts of reasons. They think that smaller and lighter boots will be more comfortable and that they give a better feel of the brake and shift levers. But mostly the reason they don't like them is because they haven't given themselves enough time to become accustomed to how they feel. The best boots on the market take a bit of getting used to. They are stiff for a reason and that is to protect your foot and ankle but even though the boots feel cumbersome to begin with they will mould to your shape after a few rides. It's a small sacrifice in comfort that will offer incredible gains in protection. The top-shelf boots will have an inner liner booty that is very comfortable and makes them easier to put on every day. Make sure they fit well and that the fastenings will prevent your boots from sliding off, and avoid any lacings that might get caught in your pegs, gears or brake pedal.

Check the MotoCAP rating on all gear before you purchase and make sure it's up to Australian standards.

So since we're talking about dresses, or rather how to dress – towards the end of the day when everyone starts to tire they start dragging the chain a bit, and I have to keep their spirits high and energy levels up to get them into camp before the sun goes down. On a day just like that my driver called me and told me that he'd picked up a struggling backpacker along the road and had brought them in to camp with him. He'd called me to ask the group's permission and check if they would mind sharing camp with the new stranger until we reached our destination. I relayed the message about the blonde, Swedish backpacker and all were very willing to share and surprisingly reinvigorated. There were no more stops until we reached camp that afternoon but I was met with a bit of disappointment when they realised that 'Stefan' was in fact German, male and didn't wear a skirt.

CHAPTER 10

Techniques

I have had quite a few journalists come on tour with me to write articles about what we do. On one particular occasion, it was the first time I'd met this rider who had come up to write about our three-day tour around Cape Tribulation and the Cooktown area, and since Jim was a good rider I gave him a treat and took him out to Cape Flattery as well. So we were heading up the road to tackle the CREB Track and all was good – we were cruising. I'd kind of sensed that Jim was competitive and wanted to challenge me in the riding skills department. Remember, I have that psychology degree to see it straight away. We got to the CREB and I opened the first gate and rode through to let him close it. I said, "See you at the next gate," which was kind of like throwing a red flag to the bull. So from the gate I took off gradually and slowly built up the pace until I was out of sight in the twists and turns. When I couldn't see Jim in the rear-view mirror I put my race face on and took off, trying my hardest to widen the gap between us. Having ridden this track hundreds of times I knew a couple of shortcuts and before I knew it I had the advantage, so

I rode like I was in the Dakar[8]. Upon getting to the next gate I quickly stripped my helmet and gear off, parked my bike next to a tree, sat down and leaned against the tree. I rolled a smoke, broke it in half – lit both, put one out and sat there as calmly as I could. Jim arrived huffing and puffing and shakily asked how long I had been there – I looked down and shuffled the butt on the ground to draw his attention to it... and said, "Well, this is me second smoke".

Having said that, I'm going to mention that that was play for me and I usually prefer to ride fast enough to stay alert and focused, but the best governance is visibility. If you can stop before you get to the end of your field of vision then you're pretty safe. Ride your own ride, don't get drawn beyond your field of vision by a faster rider nor ambling along behind a slower one, unless you're the sweep. I'm always concerned about our sweeps because it can be frustrating and you will lose focus if you're stuck in this predicament and are wondering what's for dinner – then you're not riding safe and it's time to swap that role.

Riding tips and techniques are in your face everywhere you read and none of them are wrong. They are all educating from their own experiences or training. Some riders learn from their parents at an early age and some learn from their peers much later, some are coached by professionals and some teach themselves – we're all different but enjoying the ride in any case. Like anything there are good teachers and there are bad teachers but I am sure that they come with good intentions, as I do when I offer my opinion.

If someone comes to me with a concern about their skills, the most common reason is the worry about holding up the rest of the group. I always tell them that there is nothing you can't do at your own pace. It's not like we're attempting to jump the Eiffel Tower – we're going to stick to the ground. The second concern is ego and that

---

[8] Dakar – Famous desert rally race in the USA.

TECHNIQUES

they might look a bit dicky when trying to attempt some of the sections right beside their motocross champion friends.

So let's take a look at a champion to answer this question. If you're a golfer you will know what I mean when I say that Jim Furyk has the ugliest swing in the history of professional golf but it works for him. He's got 17 tour wins, he was the PGA player of the year in 2010 and won the FedEx Cup Championship of the same year. Are we going to ridicule him because he's not elegant or are we going to applaud his accomplishments? I can tell you that my guides and I will be there to praise you for having a go. Technique, style and skill will come if you keep having a go.

Take the pressure off yourself, don't speed through your trip in an endeavour to keep up, just enjoy the ride. We've done a lot of riding in big groups and sometimes they split into two – the fast guys and the slow guys. Well guess what? The fast guys sometimes finish last because they create more crashes, punctures, riders getting lost, you name it. Slow riders don't hold a group up; riders who crash do. It is an accident that will slow the group, not a slower rider. What's a few minutes between mates? Keep a few of these examples in mind and relax.

Our corner man system

When you're riding in groups in new areas, one big concern is losing a rider in the middle of nowhere. We always explain our system over and over but it never works 100%. So let's try it here and see how we go. The guide is the lead rider and no one is allowed to pass him. We also nominate a tail or sweep rider, no one rides behind them and the group spreads out in between. At each intersection, opened gate or danger point the lead guide stops and waits for the rider directly behind him to arrive, the guide informs the second rider which direction to take, to close the gate or warn the next rider about the danger and then number two waits for the third rider while the guide gets on his way again. Two passes the batten to the third rider and gets on his way again. The rider with the batten needs to make sure the following rider clearly understand the message. No winking or blinking or nodding. It has to be a definite fist up in the air to confirm. You don't move until you see the fist up and all is well. This is to make sure that there isn't a message coming in the other direction for the lead guide; for example, the sweep rider has a flat tyre and will be late into a regroup or there's been an accident and we need the lead guide back.

Then on it goes until it reaches the sweep who closes the gate and continues on. Hopefully he puts the bike on the inside before closing the gate. I've left it on the outside before and wondered where my bike was when I tried to get on and go again…

There are other systems where the lead rider that knows the trails will go through, leaving the first rider behind him to stay on point and the pack passes through until the sweep arrives. The fella on point is usually one of the faster riders, obviously he was out front and how frustrating is it that he has to pass through, riding behind the slower riders, overtaking when safe and getting through the pack again. Not to mention that he's dusting up the rest of the pack. Our system allows each rider to find his/her place in the pack and keep it through the day. It's better to just know your place in the pack and follow through with this system. Depart from any stops or regroups in this order too.

Fixation

Fixation is a common thing, especially when you are getting mentally and physically drained. Pull up and take a break if you find yourself fixating on obstacles ahead. I know it's easy to say but

TECHNIQUES

if you don't want to hit that tree, if you don't want to hit that one rock in the middle of the road, don't look at it, because as soon as you do you will gravitate towards it. Look where you want to go – again, it sounds simple but so many riders make this mistake. They get fixated on an object and almost always hit it. Look ahead to where you DO want to go and the bike will follow automatically.

There is one particular trail which is one of the longest and most demanding rides on our tour, and it throws a continuous series of tests at the riders all day. While taking a group along it one day, I pulled up to re-group the riders. We had a bit of a break and a chat and I noticed that one of them had fallen behind, taking a bit longer than usual to reach us. So I went back to look for him and I found him sitting on the side of the track with my tail-end sweep attending to him. There were no physical injuries – he was just mentally fatigued and needed a break.

After having a chat to the attending guide and the rider I realised that he had hit the tree that we were now parked up next to. This bulldusty, rutted-out trail that we were on had taken its toll on him physically and mentally. It took me a while to work out that he'd had a different issue to the bulldust I'd assumed at the beginning and it became more obvious that he'd worked himself into a fixation. If you look at something that you don't want to hit and keep looking at it – you WILL hit it. This one particular tree was not on the trail we were riding and there were no other obstacles within 30-40 metres of it. There was just this one tree that was at least five metres off the side of the track. He'd fixated on it and sure enough that's where he landed. Look where you want to go - NOT at the ONE tree way off in yonder.

Be confident and practice looking ahead. Look as far forward as possible – in technical sections aim for at least 20-30 metres. View the ground ahead and choose the line you want to take. Pick your best line early and subconsciously you will ride over the line you have just visualised. What you see is where you go. When you are in a technical section, like a creek crossing for example, view the exit, not the ground you are covering, move forward and allow the bike to take you through.

Position and weight distribution

Rider position is the starting point for teaching any new technique or rider skill – every technique will start with this rule. Get your position right and everything else falls into place, and your riding will improve immensely. When riding in a straight section of track you should generally place your weight between the middle and the rear of the seat. The ideal is to place your weight over the rear half of the motorcycle. This distribution of weight allows the front wheel to be free floating over any obstacles and stabilises the bike at higher speeds. I say weight distribution because the position is true when you are seated or standing.

TECHNIQUES

In technical sections, for example when cornering or crossing creeks, you should move your weight forward. The rule of thumb in technical sections is to move your weight to the front half of the motorcycle. Be aware that your position is forward and that you are not just leaning forward. Your weight must be over the front wheel to be able to manoeuvre the bike. This may sound simple but, in actual fact, by moving your position forward you have actually moved your whole posture. Your legs and arms will follow and be in the right position. This shifts the weight onto the front wheel and helps you to steer and corner better. These are two basic starting rules!

Stand or sit

As I've said before, I spend a lot of time on the bike in a standing position. It's a common question that new riders will ask – about whether they should be standing or sitting for this or that. Having done so many miles on a motorcycle I am very comfortable in a standing position. I find it to be a more balanced position, allowing the bike to move freely under me while I use my knees and elbows as shock absorbers. It just gives less stress and feedback to my body and the bike does the majority of the work. But when I am on good sections of the road I will sit down to save energy, standing every now and again to stretch my legs and get the blood circulating. If you are comfortable standing up in technical sections then do so. It does feel awkward to a lot of riders, but you will become more relaxed with it as you spend more time on the bike.

Sand

Eighty percent of our riders will have trouble with sand. I've got to go there again. If you are a competent rider you can go ahead and listen to the collective advice given on how to manage sand

and that's getting the weight off the front wheel, sitting back in the saddle and keeping the throttle on. This is the most common, taught technique for sand. It's a great technique and it works well if you are out on a beach with wide open free space and nothing to hit! What about the sandy tracks that weave through trees, rocks and ruts that are created by 4WD's though? It's all well and good if you have a lot of experience and confidence to keep the throttle open in these sections but if this is your first experience with sand then this technique is irrelevant. It's near impossible for an inexperienced rider to hold the throttle open when the bike wants to climb out of or into the rut. If you don't have the experience that's ok, put your ego aside and paddle through as best you can.

I've seen riders doing the right thing, feet up on the pegs and trying their best to do what they've been told. They keep getting beat up against the edges, body slamming into the ground and physically coming off time and time again. They become exhausted, defeated, mentally and physically drained. I just can't watch these guys trying and struggling so I pull them away from the group and quietly suggest that it is ok to go in first or second gear depending on your comfort of speed, put out the outriggers (your feet) and stabilise the bike. If you're trapped in a rut stay there and paddle your way through it. Yes, it is slower and not so glamourous but you will arrive safely. This technique will get you through to the "correct" destination, not the other one. I watch hundreds of riders every year making these modest little mistakes, we repeat those two simple rules and they always improve the skill of the rider.

Beaches

Having just mentioned wide open free space with nothing to hit it's probably a good time to mention that the beach actually does have things that are going to catch you out. You can be cruising along the hard-packed wet sand and where the tides have shifted the sand there can be a two-foot step-up with a vertical edge that you just can't see. It's like being snow blind. I've seen this happen so many times, where a rider hits the step and the front digs in while the rear kicks up throwing the rider over the handlebars in the flying 'W'[9].

The tidal washouts where the current of the outgoing tide is pulling the water back in can also be a bit of a trap. They just look like the sand has a mirror top but if the water is still pulling back, what lays underneath can be a quagmire and consume a tyre, axel-deep in the blink of an eye, and if you're doing any speed you're going to sink. This is where you need to have your weight at the back of the bike to help the front wheel float over the soft sections.

I've seen a brand new Toyota Troop Carrier go into one of these and get caught. The driver walked, the tide came in and fully submerged the vehicle. It was on a remote beach location with a very difficult access that makes recovery a huge and expensive mission. I've been watching the ocean consume that vehicle for about 30 years now and there's not much left but rusted metal, chassis and wheels.

Every now and again you come across somebody who has a passion for adventure that matches your own. I have a mate like that, Glen, and every chance we get we will go and push our boundaries and explore some of the wildest areas of the Cape in search of something new. We'll research the WWII stories and go looking for wrecks or go in search of a fishing mecca or for trails that have been mentioned in historic documents. On one of these annual trips we got well caught out by the beach.

---

[9] The Flying 'W' – The rider's legs and butt form a 'W' in the air.

Our problems all started with a lithium battery that had failed on my Husaberg. I run a lithium battery because they are much lighter. A normal lead acid battery will allow the current to continue through the circuit which allows the battery to recharge if you jumpstart and run the bike. A lithium battery blocks the current running through the circuit. We found this out after several attempts to tow start it with Glen's DRZ 400.

I have to take full responsibility because this particular battery was in a previous bike and was well past its use by date. NOTE: keep a track of the date you replace batteries and check regularly so this doesn't happen to you.

There was one particular creek that we had to cross when the tide was on the way in. Our preferred camp was on the other side. This beach run had several small bays that had surrounding rock cliffs that would fill up on high tide – the beach on the other side did not. So we got to work collecting rubbish off the beach to make a raft. There was a wooden crate

TECHNIQUES

larger than average and a string of plastic buoys that would provide enough buoyancy to carry the bike. The sun was going down quick and we were working in the dark. On a last trip back for more buoys I spotlighted the little red eyes of a baby croc. Where there are babies there will be a mumma. So I looked around with the torch and spotted her red eyes glowing back at me from a fair way upstream.

We got that raft together quick smart, chucked the bike on top, walked either side of it and pushed it across the creek, one hand on the raft and one hand spotlighting Mum. We did really well until we got to the middle and deepest section of the creek. Being the short arse on this trip I was totally reliant on the raft to hold me up. Glen was taller and assured me that he had a good foot hold on the bottom and we made it to the other side but there was no relief just yet. We had to go back and get the other bike. I was useless because I couldn't even touch the ground and the tide was getting deeper.

We hustled the second run and managed to get both bikes over before the water got too deep for the both of us. We settled in for the night, set a campfire and cooked up some Barra that we'd caught earlier in the day. About two hours later I looked back to the opposite bank where we'd left from and mum croc was lying in wait for our return, which is their natural instinct.

I called the support driver that was waiting for us at our planned destination to let him know what had happened. We organised to meet him at a location that he could easily find the next day, as he was a newbie and didn't know the area well. I tried to start Glen's bike in the morning to head off and get to our support but saltwater had got in and shorted out the electrics and drained that battery as well.

So we walked, stripped off to bare feet in the sand. Along the way we came across a computer bag full of dried noodles and that was an awesome snack at the time. Glen found a thong and put it on, then he found one for the other foot and as we walked along he made upgrades wherever he found them. By the end of our journey he had a brand new matching pair of crocs that fit him. Crocs the rubber sandals, not the animals – we didn't want anything to do with the animals. With the help of the support vehicle and the time it took us to get back the bikes had dried out, and as soon as we replaced the batteries they both started with ease and off we went to the next adventure.

Overtaking

Be considerate when overtaking any car or bike. Motorcycle tyres can fling rocks and debris like you wouldn't believe, so if you are overtaking be sure to offer a wide berth to the slower rider or vehicle. Roll the throttle on steadily and get out as far as possible to overtake. Then allow as big a gap as you can before coming back in. You don't want to shower a rider in dust and rock and hamper his vision and you don't want to smash a driver's windscreen if he's likely to meet up with you at the next servo.

CHAPTER 11

The anchor

The bumbag is an essential part of any trail rider's kit. Mine has become a part of my daily attire, it's no longer an accessory for special occasions like going for a ride on the weekends and it's become more like a part of my body. I actually feel weird, like I've lost something, if it is not strapped in place. I've had it on for so long that I find it difficult to ride a motorcycle without it. The anchor keeps me on the bike and balanced oddly enough, but too many individuals rely on their mates or other riders to get them out of trouble. This is an ultimate ride-wrecker for them and it will probably ruin your day if they haven't got the tools to suit your bike.

There are tonnes of tips out there telling you how to fix a breakdown and every single one of them is useless without the right tool for the job. To match that, there are a tonne of tools to choose from. So which tools do you need and which ones just accumulate like utensils in the kitchen drawers? A bumbag should be personalised to suit the bike you're riding (check your manual) and it should be set up to suit your mechanical capabilities. A fully stocked bumbag can get really heavy so reducing weight is an important factor; think about the tools you are packing and make sure that you are not doubling up. Take spanners and tyre levers for example – these can be welded together to make one tool. This also works for two different spanners.

I never go anywhere without my bumbag. It is always within easy reach – whether I'm leading a tour group, on a fun ride, out on a boat, fixing fences or driving long distance, I never leave it behind. Renae will attest to that because it's usually at her feet in the passenger side footwell of the car. My kit is worth its weight in gold and performs like a magician's hat, all you need is a bit of common sense and it can fix just about any problem you'll encounter.

There's only been one day that I thought about letting it go: I was on a ride with a full crew of mixed-ability riders, it was the beginning of the season and we were out to be the first to the Cape in that year. I used to challenge myself in this way and defy the elements to get to the northernmost tip of Australia before anyone else could get through. I'm not sure any person ever paid attention to this conquest but myself and a few mates. We thought it was a very important endeavour and we managed to do it every year from 1993 to 1999. One of our biggest obstacles was the Jardine River crossing. The Jardine is the biggest river on the Cape York Peninsula and pumps about 2000 gigalitres of freshwater out of the catchment and into the ocean each year. It's big, it's impressive, it's home to about 46 different species of fish and it hosts about 1,000 saltwater crocodiles. The crocs are big and healthy and some are up to five metres in length. We get across on the ferry that is a flatbed, drive on/drive off boat that is attached to two cables while the motor slides it along from bank to bank. Knowing that we were early in the season and that the operators might not be in attendance I made a call to them to make sure they would be there. I've been doing this for years and had built up a good relationship with all the drivers. My group had a flight to catch and we didn't have any muck-around time to spare.

THE ANCHOR

So we rocked up at the designated time and there was no-one to be seen. We waited a while and watched the opposite side of the bank where the ferry was parked for any signs of movement. This went on for a few hours until I started to get anxious about the delay and decided to take matters into my own hands. These guys had to get to Bamaga that day! There were two empty 44-gallon drums sitting beside the ticket office that we thought would make for a good boat for me to sit on and pull myself across the cables to get to the other side. I could then drive the ferry and get my boys across. I'd had plenty of experience on boats, I'd sailed around Australia on a yacht during my travels and was confident in my skills to drive this punt.

So I set off on my makeshift raft and all was going just beautifully and I was making good time until I got to about halfway across. The flow of the river channelled in the middle and I noticed the current getting stronger because my raft started to quiver a little bit. I didn't pay much attention to it at first because I was concentrating on pulling the cable and making headway to the other side but as I got further into the channel and the current peaked to its fastest flow I found myself in full-blown speed wobbles. It was causing such a stupid rhythm that my legs started beating against the drums. It was getting out of control and threatening to throw me overboard. At this point I remembered that I was in my riding pants, I still had my boots on and my bumbag was clamped firmly around my hips – if I came off these drums I was going straight to the bottom. I had to hold the cable with both hands to stay attached, so taking anything off wasn't an option as my brain bounced off my skull with the building vibrations working their way up my body. I was certainly not ditching my bumbag because I needed it to get the ferry started. Glancing at the riders on the bank I just left and seeing the fear in their eyes was not helping. "Stick to Plan A, Roy, swimming is not an option," I thought – and that was without mentioning the dinosaurs with big teeth below. So I collected every ounce of nous and mustered all the strength in my body to calm this shit down and demand the raft to get me to the other side.

Six hours later we were riding into Bamaga Township and I saw the ferry drivers making their way in the opposite direction. I pulled them up and told them not to bother coming to collect us and what I'd just done with the ferry. They had no issues and thanked me because now they could go back to wedding they'd been attending that day.

Over the years I've learned to lessen the weight wherever possible. I've changed over to aluminium tyre levers, titanium spanners, double-ended screwdrivers with reversible shafts for a flat and Phillips head so you're not carrying two types of screwdrivers. Make sure you are carrying the right size spanners to suit your bike – for example, if you had a 12-millimetre and a 13-millimetre double-ended spanner and you are riding a Japanese bike, the 13-millimetre is useless, but if you are riding a European bike you will need the 13-millimetre because they do run a few nuts and bolts in that size. You'll need a matching socket set because some of the nuts and bolts are recessed and can't be accessed with a conventional spanner.

THE ANCHOR

I've had a lot of people work for me over the years but there were a few that were very special. Back in the early days I had a young fella who started up with us, he was a motorcycle mechanic, a gun rider and an all-round nice guy. He taught me a lot about **thinking outside of the box** instead of just relying on what we had in the toolbox. If we didn't have what we needed he would make it. For example; I needed a 10-millimetre allen key to expose the nut on the end of the crank shaft under the side cover and I didn't have one. So the young fella simply got a bolt that had a 10-millimetre hexagonal head on it and then he put two nuts on the bolt end opposite the head and locked them in together. The bolt head became an allen key and I could lever the spanner off the locked-in nuts. I was really impressed by these small but very handy tips that he shared with me and he made me a better bushman and mechanic. He worked with us for two years before he was poached by one of our riders who gave him the opportunity to move up into the head mechanic's role for a very successful international race team. I was very sad to see him go but boy was I proud to watch his career blossom in the way that it did and I couldn't be happier for him.

I call my bumbag 'the anchor' for good reason; it's heavy! I want you to keep this in mind always because, as simple as it sounds, some people forget this fact. I've worn mine for so long that I forget it is even on my body until something happens, like walking out to check the height and current in a creek crossing. If the current is strong and catches you out, the slippery surfaces underfoot can get really hard to manage very quickly and force you into the drink. Now I'm fairly quick-witted and my safety is my priority but I do think twice about letting my bumbag go. It is the thing that makes me feel safest and I'm not going to run the risk of losing it downstream! My brain does battle while I'm gurgling under water. "Do I undo the clasp, how am I going to maintain a firm grip if I do and whatever you're going to do you better do it bloody quick because we're running out of oxygen here," it says.

KING OF THE CAPE

I learned a long time ago through this experience to be very wise about where I'm carrying this anchor into. When I do remember it's there, I either take it off and leave it on my bike, or I sling it over my shoulder if I think I might need it on the other side.

So what do I have in that anchor that's worth drowning for?

1. Open-ended ring spanners
2. Sockets in quarter-inch drive, ratchet and extension bar, sizes 6, 8, 10, 12,13 and 14
3. Allen keys in sizes 3, 4, 5, 6, 8 and 10-millimetre
4. Reversible screwdriver as mentioned
5. Small flat screwdriver, just to be sure
6. Shifting spanner
7. Spoke spanner
8. Pliers
9. Spark plug socket and a spare spark plug
10. Chain-breaker and two joining links

<u>Tyres</u>

11. Tyre levers – we used to make our own by cutting it in half and welding on the spanner that fits the axel nut but you can buy these in aluminium with the ring spanner to match your bike's axel nut at the dealer.
12. 2x front tubes and 1x rear
13. Tyre patch kit as a back up
14. Bike pump and CO2 canisters
15. Front sprocket with spare nut and washer
16. Brake pads (front and rear)
    These last two might be overkill for your kit but I run tours with a lot of bikes so I have them.

THE ANCHOR

<u>Bits and Pieces</u>
17. Fuses
18. Zip ties of various sizes
19. An assortment of useful nuts and bolts (sweep the shed floor and find out what's there)
20. Quick metal
21. Small rubber bung to suit the radiator hose
22. Tow strap
23. Duct tape
24. Telescopic magnetic stick (this has a multitude of uses like finding dropped bolts in long grass)
25. Collapsible pruning saw (this is an asset when you come across fallen trees)
26. Emergency phone number list for your area (mine is laminated) – include the roadhouses and fuel stops. That comes in handy if you run out of fuel ten kilometres short of the servo.

<u>Final hints</u>
- Take the time to pack the bum-bag so that each piece has a comfortable home.
- Always check the bag before a ride.
- When using your bag of tricks always put the piece back where it came from.

It is so easy to leave things behind when you're in a rush and tools can shake loose on a ride if they are not put away properly. If it has its own place, you can visually see if something is missing and you have left it behind. This kit is not cheap to prepare and it's frustrating to restock lost pieces so pay it some respect and it will continue to get you out of strife.

Another use for an anchor: I had a club of 15 riders come up with their own bikes who chartered me to guide them through to Cape York. There was a variety of bikes ranging from a KTM 300, two stroke through to Husaberg 570's. They were all kitted out with long-range tanks and all the bling for a big trip. At the time I was riding a Husaberg 500. On the second day we came up to the Bloomfield River and after a bit of rain in the days before and overnight it was running fairly hard. It's not always the depth that's going to catch you out – this river is wide and it was running hard. At only knee-deep it was a difficult crossing because of the sheer force of the current. So I parked my bike and walked out to gauge how much pressure the water was pushing. I thought to myself that it was borderline but doable if we proceeded with caution. Being the tour guide, I am always the guinea pig and the one who goes first. So I walked the bike across while it was in first gear and used the motor to help me forward. I could feel the force of the water against the bike and I thought the front end could go at any minute. To get more traction on the front, I loaded up the front wheel by putting slight pressure on the front brake and making it bite in whilst the motor was aiding the forward movement. I got to the other side, parked the bike and walked back across to let the boys know the tip about the front brake.

They gingerly made their way across one by one. The guy on the KTM 300, two stroke was going to be an issue because he had a much lighter bike so I recommended that two people should bring this one across. When I'm on charter and all the boys have their own bike I can only make suggestions though, and he felt confident enough to go it alone. He was going well until around halfway across when the front wheel let go and both he and the bike ended up in the river, floating downstream in the rapids. The current carried him 150 metres away before we even knew he'd gone in. He held his bike below him and well underwater for the longest time until he had no choice but to let it go and swim for his own safety to the riverbank. If he'd been wearing a bumbag like mine he might have been in a whole hell of a lot of trouble.

While he was resting on the bank, gasping for air, with his boots still in the water, he met the kids from the local community. They were hanging *around playing and watching all the action, when one of them spoke up and said, "Hey mister, there's a big crocodile in there eh! We saw him yesterday!". A swim retrieval was definitely out of the question.*

There was a boat on the bank not far away so we went to find the owner and ask if we could borrow it to recover the bike from the river. He generously obliged and we took the tinny out to scout the bottom. The water was crystal clear and we could eventually see the bright orange of the KTM laying six to eight foot down below us. Obviously no one wanted to dive for the bike with a crocodile in the area so we used the anchor as a grappling hook to try to snag and drag the bike up. After a few attempts we successfully did that, strapped the bike to the side of the boat and skull dragged it back to the bank. It was a pretty simple process to de-drown it, being a two stroke, and we had it up and running in no time. The rider was ecstatic after that and gave the boat owner a sizeable tip for his generosity.

CHAPTER 12

Less is more

Exploring

In Far North Queensland, our motorcycle tours slow down at the first sign of the monsoonal wet season. I take this opportunity to go exploring new trails. Every year there's an old bushy who will tell me about 'this old track' that he remembers. The temptation to find trail riding 'gold' is too much to leave alone and the annual exploration trip begins.

The first thing we do is research the topographical maps of the area. You can get these from the lands department or a good newsagency and these help to get a clear picture of the terrain. We add any available data to the GPS, which is then attached to the bars of the bike. When exploring, the GPS is a vital piece of equipment, which is now affordable.

A lot of these unused tracks are still considered as gazetted road even though they haven't been used for years. Check with the appropriate governing authority to gain permission. These tracks could be on private property in which case you will require permission from the property owner to enter. In this day and age of 'public liability', you can ease the owner's mind by telling them that a registered vehicle on a gazetted road leaves no liability on his shoulders. Be responsible on these roads, leaving gates as you find them and taking any rubbish with you.

It's super exciting getting ready for a big adventure but the planning can be a real challenge. There's only so much space on the bike and the unknown about what to pack is daunting for most. After thousands of kilometres of off-road touring, camping and fishing, sitting around the campfire and sleeping under the stars I can offer a few suggestions to help you on your way.

Test drive your kit before you leave home. Spend some nights out in your backyard making a fire, cooking a meal and getting a good night's sleep, pack it all away again and do the same thing the following night. It's the best way to make sure you're not doubling up on something or missing an essential item.

Water

Get yourself a good-sized backpack that you're going to wear and make sure it has a bladder to carry at least two, if not three, litres of water. These bladders come with a long hose that you can tuck on the armband of the backpack and sip at your water throughout the day. Don't buy a cheap one or it's just going to split and leak all over the contents of your backpack. Save the bladder for water only, if you put anything else in there it's going to stain and be unsightly for the rest of your journey – not to mention that any sugars left in an empty bladder or hose will turn into bacteria that could cause some serious illnesses later in your trip. If you don't like the flavour of the water – isn't it funny how we all like our 'home' water best – you can get some tablet-form electrolytes that don't have the sugar content. They will mask the flavour of the 'holiday' water and provide some essential minerals. Dehydration is a very serious factor in remote areas and many riders succumb to the condition. One problem that you may not have thought about but that I see so regularly is the misuse of a three-litre camelback. Riders will be working hard, sweating profusely because they're not used to the temperature or the amount of exercise, and they drink and drink, scoffing down their water ration in the first couple of hours. This becomes really problematic at the end of the day when the pack is dry. In remote areas where water is scarce, make sure you know where the next top-up is going to be and take regular sips and ration your allowance throughout the distance. Less is more.

When I travelled the Cape as a youngster I made friends with one of the police officers, and given that there was nowhere else to stay in this little township he offered me a bed at his home for the night. It was delivery day and all the goods were stored in the lock-up so they could be distributed to the store and the pub the following day. I realised I'd been offered the bed so I could help him fetch and stack the cartons and cartons from floor to ceiling in the little room of the modestly upgraded tin shack.

When we got back in the morning there were two very happy souls almost asleep beside the commercial bin that was stored against the back wall of the watch house. Seeing bodies asleep around the neighbourhood was fairly common so the officer ignored them, unlocked the shed and we went in. It was brighter than the day prior and we could immediately see a few extra spotlights of sunshine coming through the roof. It turns out that these young fellas had a great night cutting holes in the roof and drinking all the beers they could reach before cutting another hole and fishing it out before cutting another hole…so don't let yourself get so thirsty that you can't think anymore. If it had have been me, I would have cut one big hole, grabbed the lot and taken off so I wouldn't get caught.

Clothing

This is what I will pack for any amount of days; three t-shirts and shorts, invest in some nylon or micro-fibre styles that have moisture-wicking and quick-dry notes on the label – don't pack bulky fabrics – one pair of tracky dacks and a jumper. I also have a down puffer jacket that takes up a minimal amount of room. Any of these new technologies that pack small and are highly functional are best. Remember that you have your riding jacket as another layer if it's required at night to keep warm. Jocks – test them and make sure they aren't going to cause any issues in those sensitive areas, again quick dry microfiber or even bamboo. Don't go overboard and pack one for each day, just get better at keeping a secret. Two pairs of thick socks, the best quality you can afford. There is nothing worse than blisters or foot rot when you're out on a ride, it just makes everything a miserable experience. Then either a pair of sneakers or thongs, not both. I prefer a combination sandal that covers all bases. Microfiber clothing is comfortable to wear with their moisture-wicking properties to keep you dry in hot or wet climates – they will pack smaller, are tougher, stain-resistant and they don't hold odours. They're lightweight and can be washed in a small basin at a roadhouse, in the shower with you or in the creeks when you have a swim.

Just be mindful that the soap you are using on your clothes and yourself is environmentally safe. An all-in-one, natural, oil-based, hard soap will wash your clothes, hair, body and dishes, so it's a good option. The same goes with any sunblocks, lotions and potions. Please take a moment to do the right thing – we are all coming into these areas because they are beautiful and we want to keep them that way. Pack some biodegradable toilet paper and make sure it's buried deep to help it break down quicker and stop the animals from digging it up. There's nothing worse to see in a remote campground than someone else's TP.

One small towel; get yourself an ultralight chamois towel from a camping store that packs small and dries out overnight.

Invest wisely in a pair of really good sunglasses – get the polarised ones because vision is seriously important out on the bike and it helps to spot the fish more easily. You will be going through ever-changing lighting conditions when you're trail riding, especially in the forests where the trees block and release the sunlight like a strobe light is going off.

I always have a small torch and a lighter in with my clothes – you never know what you might need it for. Insect repellent is also a good idea to have on hand – again choose an environmentally-friendly brand.

Less is not always more when it comes to clothing. I have a driver who likes to take his gear off at any opportunity, usually after a few bevvies when somebody has opened up the conversation he'll bring out the tackle with some random story about the family jewels. He's a funny bastard and everyone loves him but you better pray he doesn't find out that it's your birthday. He's a good cook and wears an apron to work the campfire, it's got big pockets to hold his torch and tools. He'll even bake you an awesome cake in a camp oven. Then he will bring you up to the table and stand you out front of the on-looking crowd. He'll go off to collect your cake, deliver it back to you with his back to the crowd and it'll be all about you. He makes you feel very special. Then he bends over to light your candles and the whole crowd starts hollering with joy, they dive for their cameras and the birthday boy is delighted, smiling like the Cheshire Cat – right up until he sees the photographs of the cook's bare naked bum leaning over the table. It's memories like these that last a lifetime.

Camping and cooking

Our camping kit is made up of a lightweight, synthetic, micro sleeping bag (for ten degree temperatures), and a compact inflatable pillow which we roll up in an inflatable air mattress that gets wrapped in a tarp and hooky strapped to the rear guard of the bike. At night if it is going to rain then the tarp is going to keep you dry. Well, as dry as you can hope for, so keep in mind that these items need to be quick-drying also. You don't want to be climbing into a sleeping bag that is still damp from the night before. Pack according to your weather conditions.

We carry a satellite telephone – don't forget to take the phone numbers that you are likely to use, for example; emergency services, national park ranger stations, local service stations and any station homesteads that you will be near. I keep these numbers laminated in my bumbag.

It's always a good idea to carry a basic first aid kit and keep your first aid knowledge updated. We do a remote area and wilderness course and our basic first aid regularly to keep that part of our brains ticking over on the latest information available.

Food

I pack a three-piece telescopic fishing rod. You can add to the adventure by living off the land, eating bush tucker. If you're out on the beaches keep your eyes open and you'll be able to find a feed, the rocks have oysters and the holes in the sand could be hiding a mud crab. Most creeks will have something to offer, either fish or yabbies or cherubin. Get to know your local native fruit trees too, we have Davidson plums, lemon aspen which is great on fish and the list goes on. We pack minimal food for backup such as energy bars and small cans of tuna or baked beans. Never bash the baked beans! I actually lived for weeks on a can a day when I travelled around Australia on a dime.

Roy's crazy damper – not crazy Roy's damper

Mix 4 cups of self-raising flour, with a cold beer and a half – drink the other half while you mix it up to a damp dough, chuck in a bag of dried fruit mix, a tablespoon of cinnamon and a half a cup of sugar. Oil the camp oven and bung in the dough lid on and let it sit while you have another beer. Then place a shovel load of coals beside and close to the burning fire, sit the camp oven on top, place another shovel of coals on the lid and let it cook for about 20-30 minutes and there you go – dessert is served.

As you've probably gathered I love my fishing and so do most of my guides, so at the end of each season we take the opportunity to do a fishing trip and I'll share my secret spots with those that are keen. On this particular trip the driver, lead guide and I went out to one of my favourite spots. Fishing is a competitive sport and we were all talking it up about who was going to catch the biggest and the most fish. We got out to the coast, at the mouth of the river where it always produces. At our precise arrival time the water was active and teaming with fish. There was a massive boil, birds working and fish jumping – it was totally ON. The competition had begun and we were all champing at the bit and casting away frantically. As soon as my line hit the water I hooked up and landed a 60-centimetre barra, the lure flew back into the water and hooked up again. This went on all afternoon and I just couldn't miss.

The boys didn't have near the same luck and they couldn't work out what was going on. They had the same lure, same rods and the same casting area but didn't have the hook-up rate that I had. I won the day and we were sitting around the fire having a few beers when they had to ask and I let the secret out of the bag. We have several fishing rods and tackle boxes on tour so the ones I gave to the boys I had sprayed with WD40.

Sharp-tooth saw

No, you do not need this for my damper but for the unused tracks that go wild quickly and often have fallen trees. We started carrying fold-down handsaws for clearing the trail at the beginning of each season but we found countless other reasons to have them, for example cutting a branch to make a splint or a tripod leg to change a flat. These little saws are so handy that they have become a permanent part of the kit.

Don't forget to zip-tie a spare key somewhere on the bike or in your gear. Make sure it is hidden well but don't forget where you hide it. We are losing ignition keys all the time. The riders will put them in their pocket, go into a pub for a beer, go for a shower and change, go for dinner and into their room or tent for the night, get up the next day and get on the bike and BOOM, we spend an hour retracing his steps and everywhere in between.

Take all the necessary precautions and make sure someone knows your plan A, B and C, and that they have the same phone number list as you do. Decide before you go how often you will call in and decide beforehand what the time frame is going to be if the 'alarm' needs to be raised. Exploring new tracks is what trail riding is all about, don't sit there and complain that you have nowhere to go – go and find it yourself and have fun along the way. When you find 'gold', call me!

I met a couple who live in Cape York and they totally represent the meaning of less is more for me. They have built a shack out of their beachcombing finds and when I met them had young children. Their home had a dirt floor and one zig-zag wall that purely created some protection from the elements. This was open-plan living in its most natural form. The tin roof stood above varied girths of tree trunk posts and from every angle you could see out into the wild environment. The kitchen sink was created from flotsam and jetsam with hand-carved timber benches and tables, with scattered un-matching chairs; hand-carved chairs, milk crates with cushions and a few camp chairs to make it cosy and comfortable. The bedroom was distinguishable by the mosquito net that hung and surrounded the beds. The shower was outdoors and the bathtub was a cut-out 44-gallon drum with welded on legs that sat perched over a fire for the luxury of warmth. Renae felt uncomfortable about boiling our children in it but thoroughly enjoyed the novelty activity of getting our camp-coated creatures clean. Everything solid had been built over time from what the beach and river system had delivered. They had amazing and practical gardens that produced herbs, spices, fruit, nuts and vegetables for the family to eat alongside the catch of the day. There was a collection of free range birds to deliver eggs, and a few cows for milk.

We shared a dinner with them one night. We wanted to provide the luxuries of a steak dinner and had brought provisions. They were very excited to accept our cold beer, chocolate, chips and soft drink. They were prideful in generosity in equal measure and the whole visit was a welcome education for my children.

They made an annual trip into town to buy bags of flour and rice and whatever else they deemed essential to have for the following year. The man of the house used to hand carve wildlife statues to sell for their income and they were so lifelike that they were once raided for hunting endangered animals. He'd spend so much time working on his art pieces that his natural sweat and body oils would bring out the depth of colour in the timber and make it appear to be polished. I could go on and on about the things this couple have achieved but I'm just going to say what an inspiration they were to me over the years.

CHAPTER 13

Lifelines

 There are so many ways to be creative when it comes to survival and one of my drivers told me this story of one of his journeys. Jack lived in WA but worked for us in Cairns during the season, and at the end of it he would drive his trusty Landcruiser back home for Christmas and visit all his family and friends. He always took the most direct route via the Plenty Highway and the Gun Barrel Highway. On this expedition Jack came across a group of locals broken down on the side of the road just outside of their community. Being an experienced mechanic by trade and a very handy bushman, he stopped to offer assistance. He had all of his tools on board and was pretty sure he could fix almost anything, but the group insisted that the motor was beyond repair. Jack tried to take a look a couple of times but the crowd were all in agreement and firmly fixed on getting a tow into town. They were in a very remote location and he couldn't leave them there, so he obliged and towed them back into the community. Upon arriving in town he pulled into the service station and they all fell out of the car with such amusement and laughter and joyfully thanked him for the lift. Jack was surprised when they all walked *away down the street to the pub. That's when the servo assistant told him that the car didn't even have a motor in it and this was just their way to have a bit of fun with the tourists and get towed around from place to place without it costing a cent.*

Safety can be a real concern when you're travelling in remote parts of the world that you haven't been before. We had one particular rider from the UK who was overly sensitive about his safety. Bobby had read all about Australia and how everything wanted to kill you; the sharks, the snakes, the spiders, the crocodiles, the cassowaries etc. He asked me questions about every single one of these and I wondered why he'd came out here in the first place. Bobby made his bed twice at night, once to put it up and again before he got in, shaking the shit out of everything and shining a torch into every dark little corner checking for anything that might move or crawl. He asked at every sign of water if there was a crocodile in there and this includes the rather small puddles that form on the road.

We were a few short kilometres from camp one afternoon when I spotted a large python making its way across the road. I stopped and picked it up so it wouldn't get run over by the traffic, particularly the riders following along behind. I showed the snake to each of the riders as they came through one by one and pointed them in the direction of camp where the support vehicle was already set up. Last to come through was our chap Bobby and I couldn't resist the urge to stir him up a little. I dropped my bike on its side and laid down next to it with the python across my chest. He came in slow and I could see that he was concerned that I'd hurt myself and was going to do everything in his power to help me. He was almost stopped when he saw the snake wrapped around my arm and me holding his head away from my face. I acted it up a bit and flapped my legs and made a few sounds of distress. I'd never seen anyone look that scared or ride off so fast, he dropped that bike into gear, showering me with rocks and gravel as he took off and I'm not sure how he got his legs so high that they were above the handlebars. It occurred to me that if I had been in a serious situation, he'd just left me for dead. He got into camp shouting for help and telling the cook what had happened and the whole camp roared in laughter as cookie explained that I was pulling a prank and that it was just a python.

I'm always researching and trying to improve our tours, particularly when it comes to improving safety, so when mobile telephones came out we were one of the first to get one. It's pretty funny to look back and think about the size of that thing, it was like a brick in my backpack. It was a blessing when we were close to town. Renae and I remember lovingly the day we took our first booking while we were out on the boat fishing. She was in the boat talking on the mobile brick while I was in the water spearing crayfish and we thought we were the luckiest people on the planet in that moment. It was a sturdy beast too. I left it on the roof or the bonnet of the car several times but this one day when I was dropping a friend off to the airport, I drove away, it slid off the roof and hit the bitumen, I reversed to pick it up, ran over it – feeling the speed bump – and swore at myself, but it didn't even have a scratch on it. It was useless out on the trail as reception hadn't caught up with this new technology yet but I continued to carry it anyway.

Then we moved forward into satellite communications and had one of the first to be fitted into a vehicle that was traveling through Cape York. It was huge and very expensive but I really wanted to have it in our support vehicle. It was fitted to the back wall of the Hilux extra cab and with the steel casing that we'd engineered to protect the bulky black box, it took up half of the extra cab. That year it came in very handy for everyone else but us. We came across a few situations where the police, the ambulance and other tour operators needed to use it and it was well worth the investment.

Even though technology is improving all the time and mobile phone reception has come along in leaps and bounds, the Cape is still a very remote place with loads of drop out zones where reception just doesn't exist. A lot of the roadhouses have a superman box and all the boys pick numbers to get in the queue to call home and check-in with their wives or loved ones. One particular day comes to mind when I think about those pay phones.

These roadhouses are a collective stop for fuel, food and a beer if you need one. There are tables and bench seats for the boys to have their lunch beside the gardened fence line that separates food from fuel. Mrs. Owner had been watering the garden when we arrived and had left the hose in place to come in and serve up the lunches to the boys. The pay phone is over in the corner with a nice shady tree protecting it from the sun and a little way down Mr. Owner has mechanical storage sheds. So on this one particular day, the guides were fuelling up the bikes one after the other while the riders enjoyed their lunch and our international rider visiting from the USA was first into the booth. He was chatting away when someone yelled, "Hey that hose is moving". All hell broke loose and before anyone had uttered the word 'snake', the owner was out with a riffle taking pot shots. I looked over to our American tourist and he had a finger in his ear and the phone crammed up to the other trying to continue his conversation and when the ringing echo died down we heard him say, "What, oh they're just shooting a snake!". Well that made me giggle, I wonder what his wife thought about his vacation choices. What's funnier is the snake got away and the owner offered a free beer to anyone who could catch it and the previously nervous group of boot-clad bike riders were more aggressive than the bloody snake.

These days we carry a very compact satellite phone on the bike and we also have one in the support vehicle. They are much more efficient and cheaper than they used to be. You may not want to go out and purchase a satellite phone outright but you can now hire them from the telecommunications stores for the duration of your trip.

There are a variety of Global Positioning Systems (GPS) these days, however I am currently using the Hema maps app on my iPhone.

LIFELINES

This app gives your smartphone the ability to pick up from satellites and track your position. It allows you to zoom in and the further you zoom in the more detail you will see, and it also provides topographical maps. You can mount your iPhone to the bars for a bigger screen instead of the GPS's that have smaller screens.

If you're travelling alone, invest in a spot navigator. They are great for when you are outside normal mobile range. You can pre-set messages to friends and family and send an 'A, OK' message with the click of a button or an SOS if you get into trouble. It will send your GPS location to emergency services and responders will come to the beacon call.

Having your lifelines in place are seriously important because you just never know when you might need them. I've told you about our quests to be the first to the Cape earlier but that one was pretty tame compared to the last one we did in 1999. On this particular year we made the attempt with a small group of advanced riders. The wet season lingered longer than it had in previous years and the rivers were still quite swollen. Regardless, we wanted to be first to the Cape and we thought it would just add to the adventure of it all.

The support vehicle came along as far as Archer River where we had to leave it and its satellite telephone behind. The rivers ahead were just too high and there was no chance that it could get across. We'd stuffed our backpacks with everything that we needed from the truck and I made arrangements with a few of the ranger stations and cattle stations to accommodate us for the rest of the trip.

We'd stayed the night at the roadhouse and used the station owner's tinny to float the bikes across to the northern side bank in the morning. We headed off feeling successful and bulletproof. Not long afterward we came up to the first dip. It's normally dry and I hardly recognised the raging torrent that was chest-deep. We had to take a dip if we wanted to keep going, so we took most of our gear off and cut up some good strong sticks to put through the wheels of the bikes. Four men to a bike and we gave it a little chariot ride across the water. We turned back and did that for each bike. I looked around at the group to get a feel for the vibe and all I saw was exuberant excitement. They were high fiving each other and loving it. Off we go again!

Within two kilometres we found the next dip and repeated the same process. This went on and on and the novelty started to wear off, especially when they realised how much further we had to go. We got into our destination of Bramwell Station on dark, thoroughly exhausted but happy. There was no one else at the station because the owners and all staff had all exited the region for the wet season. It's an eerie place to be when no one is home. They'd given me directions on how to open up our accommodations and with a warm shower, full belly and soft beds we felt like kings.

The next day we took off north. Little did we know we were heading into a tropical depression, just a few notches down from a cyclone so not a lot of wind but bucketloads of rain was headed straight for us. Multiple sections of the road forward turned into full blown rivers for as far as you could see. It made for an interesting ride, not being able to see what was under the water. We couldn't see the edge of the road for one and then you'd fall into a hole or bump into a rock – it wasn't all that deep but the security of visual perception was gone. It was the blind leading the blind and we were all driving by feel. We eventually got to the Jardine River ferry and I knew two things; it wasn't operating at that time of the year and I was not going to make a raft out of 44 barrels. Instead, I had another plan – I'd get my friend who lives up the tip to motor his boat down the coast and up the mouth of the Jardine River to ferry us to the other side. Great plan but he didn't show up.

After a few hours wait I got concerned for his safety and ours, so I left the boys at the ticket booth for shelter and rode back through the 160-kilometre river to the ranger station to make a phone call. My mate is a very experienced skipper who had done this trip plenty of times in the past and he told me that he nearly ran out of fuel. I was shocked to hear this, but he explained that he had packed what he thought was going to be enough but the sheer force of going against the current of the Jardine River had consumed way more than anticipated. He'd had to turn back to make it home safely himself. He assured me that he would be there the next day. I rode back to the boys and we bunkered down for the night at the Jardine Hilton, AKA the ticket booth.

The boat coming up the river the next morning was a very pleasing sight and we started the process of ferrying the bikes to the northern bank. When we got to what was supposed to be the other side there was no dry land. We continued putting through the tree line where the road lay beneath us until we came across a road sign that read, "Ferry 1 KM" and we continued along for another 500 metres or so. The river had swollen beyond its banks by a kilometre and a half. When we did get to dry land there was a 2.5m crocodile sitting on the bank but he scooted back into the water as we arrived. Now of course we made our destination but a quest like that needed a name and it was dubbed the Poseidon Adventure.

Never give up!

KING OF THE CAPE

Afterword

Throughout this book I have been telling you about things that have occurred over 30 years and I haven't always had the knowledge or education that I have now. Policies and acceptable behaviours have changed a lot since I started riding, so I would like to do a recap on the behaviours that we follow through with in this day and age of political and social acceptability. We are all responsible for protecting our natural and cultural heritage and for raising awareness about respecting our environments and communities.

Cape York Motorcycles was the world's first motorcycle tour company to be Eco-Certified with Ecotourism Australia and we have maintained that for more than ten years, which is longer than most businesses survive. We have done this by following a few simple rules.

Research your destination before you leave home and seek permits if they are necessary. Always choose the hardened path unless it is impractical or dangerous to do so. Try not to create new tracks if you don't have to and ride gently where you can, avoiding excess wheel spin for no reason and think about protecting the trails from unnecessary erosion.

When camping, try to use designated camping areas where possible and be gentle with the environment when you can't. Keep your footprint small and try to use exposed areas where you can – don't just plonk your tent anywhere, think about the vegetation. Use gas stoves when you can and if you're going to light a fire make sure you have permission to do so. Be responsible, use what you need and think about the resources for the next person and only use fallen timber. Make sure you put it out with water if you have spare, otherwise with a layer of sand or dirt before you leave. Make campsites well away from the water's edge if you're in croc country. Always use environmentally friendly and biodegradable liquids and soaps and keep them well away from the waterways – don't take them into the water itself. Take everything you brought with you and leave the site better than before you came. Leave behind what you find unless it's not supposed to be there.

Respect the wildlife, be as quiet as you can in sensitive areas and never feed the animals – no matter how cute and fluffy they are, your snack could kill them. Beware of any dangerous species that might be in the area you are travelling.

Try to represent our brotherhood and be a good example! Stay tidy in little townships, rack your bikes up in a neat row – don't just take over a carpark and leave your bike in the middle of a thoroughfare. That's a real pet hate of mine and I see it all the time. Respect and acknowledge the locals, you're in their home. Respect and acknowledge other road users, you don't own the trail no matter how many times you've been there. Stay right away from horses, move slowly and get out of the way, make eye contact with the rider and check for any hand signals they may be giving you.

AFTERWORD

So let's do one final recap;

1. Plan your trip; we have a trip planner available at www.capeyorkmotorcycles.com.au/ourstore.
2. Get a good map of the area you will be travelling and check the weather.
3. Be honest and know your limitations, ride safely, respectfully and use some common sense.
4. Customise your bike to suit you and the ride, pack light, pack right.
5. Talk to people along the way.

And last of all, have an awesome adventure.

About the Author

Roy Kunda grew up in the outer suburbs of Melbourne, Victoria, Australia, with his parents and two younger sisters. He spent a lot of time with his dog, Sacha, hunting rabbits in the paddocks, until he discovered the other boys riding motorcycles out in the bushlands behind the budding housing estates near South Morang.

Roy started riding one of his new mates' bike in the afternoons after school and hiding his cuts and abrasions from his parents at night. He bought his first motorcycle, a Yamaha YZ80 D, at 13 years of age with money he'd earned mowing lawns. He hid it from his dad in a nearby friend's garage.

After his parents worked out that the constant gravel rash and injuries were not explained by Roy's tales they eventually got to the bottom of the story. They weren't thrilled by Roy's craving for riding and so they decided to use motorcycling as a goal setting tool to make Roy work harder for his grades at school. For every goal he reached they supported him with new riding gear or new motorcycles at the end of the year. His dad would eventually drive him to race meetings and trail riding areas.

Trail riding became a passion for Roy and he spent all his spare time around the northern part of Melbourne; King Lake, Whittlesea and Flowerdale. The appetite for adventure grew while he watched documentaries made by Alby Mangles and Malcolm Douglas. Their trips into remote and exotic locations inspired Roy to research his dream of one day doing it for himself and exploring the outback on a motorcycle.

Roy had a map of Cape York on his bedroom wall, and he visualised and worked towards that goal to travel around Australia planning and mapping all the old stock routes around Australia. Cape York was yet to be confirmed as his ideal destination but he was already thinking of starting tours there before he'd even left Melbourne.

The day after his 21st birthday Roy Kunda packed up his trusty Yamaha Tenerè and headed off. He set out with a couple of friends and the group made their way through Broken Hill and Silverton in South Australia, to hit the first stock routes – 'The Oodnadatta Track' and 'The Birdsville Track'.

After Birdsville they made their way across to the east coast and up to Far North Queensland and Cairns. This was Roy's first impression of what became his forever home. The beauty of the area and the tropical lifestyle fed his desires to be outdoors and it far exceeded his expectations. The group stayed in Cairns for a few months picking up odd jobs to replenish their funds and headed off again. Roy knew he would be back very soon.

CYMCA (Cape York Motorcycle Adventures) was the first full-time motorcycle tour operation to begin in Australia. Roy was told a thousand times not to turn his hobby into a business and that it would NEVER work. Despite that, Roy Kunda (who looks remarkably like Robert De Niro) ran his first customer ride to the Cape in 1990 and he's been humming up and down that wild frontier

ABOUT THE AUTHOR

ever since, clocking up at least 20,000km a season. The masses of riders wanting to tick the bucket list item of Cape York off their lists just keep coming to the northern-most point of the Australian mainland and they show no signs of slowing down.

Cape York Motorcycle Adventures is a family business. Renae Kunda has been by Roy's side every step of the way running the administration, creating policies that didn't exist and finding the market that worked for the company. His son Jordan joined the company after completing an apprenticeship in Mechanics and spent a year in administration before he was allowed to begin his tour guide training. Jordan is an exceptional tour guide with the patience of a saint and he's pretty handy on a guitar around the campfire too.

They operate fully guided off road tours from Cairns to the northernmost tip of the Australian continent – Cape York – where the riders can experience the best off road trails the Cape has to offer and it is the real adventure for any motorcyclist. The company was the world's first motorcycle tour company to become Eco Certified and it is a credit to them to have maintained it for over ten years. They have won multiple business and tourism awards. The business accesses National Parks, private properties, secluded swimming holes, secret fishing spots and much more. CYMCA has a varied range of tours to suit any budget or time frame. Designed to test the rider's skill level, it is the best motorcycle adventure you'll find – customers ride and CYMCA takes care of the rest.

Roy's experience, accompanied by his vast knowledge of the region, mechanical expertise, amazing riding ability and gift with people, has led to the growing success of CYMCA and what this man doesn't know about the Cape just isn't worth worrying about. Roy looks forward to slowly stepping back from the day-to-day operations of the business and handing the reins over to his son

Jordan to continue the legacy. He has no desire to retire and looks forward to many more years in the saddle. He is more likely to be spending his time exploring new destinations and creating new experiences to add to the business. 2021 will see the addition of Cairns to Darwin tours and Roy is very excited to explore and provide new tour offerings as he creates them.

Image by "Highlights Photography"

ABOUT THE AUTHOR

Roy Kunda can be contacted through Cape York Motorcycle Adventures;

Postal: PO BOX 1006, Smithfield, QLD 4878 Australia

Email: roy@capeyorkmotorcycles.com.au

Telephone: +61 (0)7 4055 0050

Mobile: 0427 590 221 (Renae's)

Web: https://capeyorkmotorcycles.com.au/

Facebook: https://www.facebook.com/CapeYorkMotorcycleAdventures

Instagram: https://www.instagram.com/capeyorkmotorcycles/

YouTube: https://www.youtube.com/channel/UCPL_9HUe0k5RqF2uNMeG9MQ

Testimonials

I booked a Cape York eight-day ride for myself and five mates through Renae. She went out of her way to offer advice and accommodate us. The ride itself was everything we had hoped for and more, Roy and his team including our gourmet bush chief Westie were fantastic. I can't recommend Cape York Motorcycles Adventures enough, don't get sucked into going with any of the other imposters, there is a reason Roy and Renae have been doing this for 30 years.

Mark Binney.

The first time I met Roy at Moreton Telegraph Station, it was all about the Cape. I can't believe he can remember all the stories, and keep having more adventures to tell. Talk about living the dream! Enjoy the ride, I know I have. Thanks mate!

Graham Blake.

"I went on a three-day trip with Roy in 2015. I was coming from Korea but I had a US drivers licence. He asked me if I could switch days over email, but unfortunately I couldn't and my trip was planned. That would leave me with a huge hole. He thought I was coming from the States so he took me on a one-on-one tour. He informed me he doesn't normally do that because they lose money with only one person signing up, but I am extremely grateful he did. This was an amazing experience. He also took a greenhorn – although I had my motorcycle license he still took me. I will tell you what, these are the highest ranked vacation memories ever. Whenever I tell stories about vacations, the stories about this tour are always first to come out. And they are some thrilling stories!

Jacob Brumaghin.

I went on a trip with my Dad and Roy a few years ago which was one of the most fun and memorable experiences I've had. It was an awesome bonding experience and we saw some of the most beautiful parts of Australia. He knows the country really well and knows lots of hidden places to visit. He was also great at adapting to any situation, we were impressed with the trackside maintenance on the bikes. We had good laughs the whole way along, probably nothing better than a week of riding bikes by day, cracking a cold beer at night and enjoying good company. Hopefully get an opportunity to go all the way up to the Cape another time!

Andrew Klink.

Me and my son Charlie recently did the Cairns to Cape York dirt bike trip. It was an amazing bonding experience for us, the ever-changing country was beautiful and reminded me why I love Australia. The boys Roy, Jeremy, and Westy made the whole experience humble, all round fun with a great professional attitude. The camps are special and so was the banter. Me and Charlie had a ball.

Chef James Watson.

Highly recommend Roy and his team – seamlessly organised a trip with 11 blokes and it was an incredible experience from the first email to the last km. The riding through the Daintree and Cape Trib speaks for itself, bloody epic, and Roy and Jeremy were amazing hosts and guides. We'll be back!

Elliot Waldron.

It was that opportunity, the one I couldn't resist when the "best job in the world" came up for grabs.

Soon to come was the most awesome six months of my life, touring the cape alongside Roy, his son Jordy and master chef Westy. In that time we showed over 100 Riders how beautiful Cape York really is! Can't wait to get back.

Regards, Jeremy Coatman.

www.capeyorkmotorcycles.com.au

PRE - RIDE CHECKLIST

AVAILABLE FOR DOWNLOAD ON OUR WEBSITE STORE:
www.capeyorkmotorcycles.com.au/our-store/

- Riding Gear
- Fluids
- Air Filter
- Wheels
- Brakes
- Controls
- Electrical
- Safety Plan
- Bumbag and Backpack

 /CapeYorkMotorcycleAdventures

 capeyorkmotorcycles

 Cape York Motorcycles

Got Questions about your Ultimate Adventure?

Got Questions about your Ultimate Set-up?

Ever dreamed of stepping onto a motorcycle and heading into the great unknown? What's holding you back?

While so many people dream about hitting the road on the adventure of a lifetime, the sad fact is that most people never do.

Is there one thing Roy can help with that will get you on your way?

YOUR DREAM ADVENTURE BEGINS TODAY!

NEED HELP?

Check out our store for a comprehensive video series.

Roy Kunda has been adventure seeking for over 35 years, he's done the miles, met all walks of life, seen all skill levels and abilities and test ridden 100's of bikes.

Let Roy share his unparalleled knowledge of the industry so you can have the time of your life and come home safely to tell the tales.

Website
www.capeyorkmotorcycles.com.au/our-store/

Email for more details:
adventures@capeyorkmotorcycles.com.au

IMAGINE 3 DAYS WITH AN EXPERT?

The 3 day MASTERCLASS will get you on your way to being an adventure riding expert.

While so many people dream about hitting the road on the adventure of a lifetime, the sad fact is that most people never do. Roy is here to help BECAUSE he has been adventure seeking for over 35 years, he's done the miles, met all walks of life, seen all skill levels and abilities and test ridden 100's of bikes.

Let Roy share his unparalleled knowledge of the industry through the 8 ULTIMATE learning modules.

DO YOU WANT AN ULTIMATE ADVENTURE?

DO YOU WANT TO KNOW WHERE TO START?

BOOK YOUR ADVENTURE RETREAT TODAY!

 https://capeyorkmotorcycles.com.au/our-store/

adventures@capeyorkmotorcycles.com.au

YOUR DREAM JOURNEY'S START HERE!

KING OF THE CAPE MASTERCLASS
3 DAY ADVENTURE RETREAT

ADVENTURE MODULES	RETREAT PLANNER
Pre-ride Planning and Logistics	●
Motorcycle Choices and Set-up	●
Bumbag set-up	●
How to use the tools	●
Riding Gear choices	●
What to Pack	●
Riding Techniques/ Improve your skills	●
Bush Mechanics	●

RETREAT PACKAGE 1
2 nights camping from your bike
Campfire meals

RETREAT PACKAGE 2
2 nights Luxury Accommodation
Restaurant meals

MENTORING
4 x 30 minute Calls
Unlimited e-mail support
Online Video support

Notes

KING OF THE CAPE

NOTES

www.ingramcontent.com/pod-product-compliance
Lightning Source LLC
Chambersburg PA
CBHW021150080526
44588CB00008B/287